PUZZLE PIECES

A JOURNEY THROUGH DEPRESSION &
OVERCOMING THE STRUGGLE OF SOCIETY

BY
JOSHUA GASKELL

Copyright © 2021 Joshua Gaskell

All rights reserved. This book or any portion thereof may not be reproduced or used in any manner whatsoever without the express written permission of the publisher except for the use of brief quotations in a book review.

Published by Mind and Body World Publishing:
www.mindandbodyworld.com

Cover by Bespoke Design and Print: www.bespoke-group.co.uk

Cover images by Gareth Roy Photography: www.garethroyphotography.com

ISBN: 9798533332668

I dedicate this book to anyone who has struggled, is struggling or may one day struggle with mental health issues. Keep fighting the battle each day.

"People can take everything away from you, but they can never take away your truth. But the question is, can you handle mine?"
—Britney Spears

CONTENTS

Chapter One 1
Chapter Two 12
Chapter Three 22
Chapter Four 32
Chapter Five 43
Chapter Six 56
Chapter Seven 64
Chapter Eight 75
Chapter Nine 88
Chapter Ten 101
Chapter Eleven 114
Chapter Twelve 130
Chapter Thirteen 149

INTRODUCTION

It's April 2021, and a week until I will be going back to work after having four months off due to the Covid-19 pandemic. This lockdown has been incredibly difficult, and I've experienced one of the lowest periods of my life, and believe me, that is saying something. I decided in mid-January that I needed some help with this battle and returned to my therapist, Catherine Shaw. After attending five sessions with Catherine (Cathy), we came up with the idea of possibly writing my journey down for others, going right back to the very beginning and discussing and reflecting on where I was, how I was and why I am. This won't be easy for me. This life hasn't been the typical 25-year-old's. I'm a young lad who has been through quite a variety of experiences. By no means am I saying I've had things the worst. There are thousands, hundreds of thousands, even millions more people who have had tougher, more challenging experiences, more chaotic times and more pain than I could even imagine and I wouldn't even like to bring up any comparisons between us. But this is my truth, this is my story, and this is why I am here.

    I'm starting this journey, sitting in the conservatory at the back of my home. I'm watching my husband. It still feels very alien to call him my husband, but in October 2020, that became official. He's putting the shopping away (somehow during this pandemic, we've managed to afford our weekly shop, another aspect where we have been very lucky, although I have had to sacrifice splurging money on nonessentials such as my weekly bacon frazzles treat) with the dogs, all three of them (Yes, we have three dogs. Three Cocker Spaniels: Albus, Aurora and Amos) all walking around by his feet waiting for any slight item to drop to the floor so they can investigate. I'm wondering to myself, is this my conclusion? Is this the happy ending? The husband, the house, the dogs? The answer is, who the fuck knows? After attending my therapy session with Cathy this morning, I'm ok with that. Life isn't about "what's next?" "Is this it?" "Is this the meaning of life?" Life is now.

I have spent the last ten years, maybe more, definitely more actually, wondering where my life was going. When will I be happy? At one point, I accepted I wasn't going to die old. I sadly accepted that I would probably commit suicide at an early age one day leaving behind a grieving family, grieving parents and grieving friends. I wondered would I be all over people's social media, "he was such a lovely boy", "he always tried to make everyone laugh", "we had no idea he was struggling". The typical statements you see when a local teen/young adult is taken away too early. At one point, I definitely had fantasies about the idea of this. Who would be sad? Who wouldn't care? Who would feel guilty? Who would go to the funeral? Obviously, my parents, my brothers, my close relatives and friends, but what about those that knew they could have done more, those that didn't really like me and what about those that didn't make my life that easy, would they attend or grieve out of guilt?

But I'm here, and who knows, maybe one day all that will be happening, I won't ever take away from myself that option because life has a funny way of working. But for now, I'm here, I'm battling through and I'm surviving.

I'm Joshua Gaskell and this is my story.

CHAPTER ONE

Wigan is a small town near Manchester, dating back to the 7th century and is most well known for its rugby team, its football team, Uncle Joe's Mint Balls and "pie eaters". The Wigan Borough had a population of around 300,000 at the time, I was very lucky to be born into The Finch Family. I was born on 20th May 1995 at Billinge Hospital, which is no longer here, at 03.08 pm. Originally my name was going to be Ellis Joshua Finch, but my parents decided to change this to Joshua Ellis Finch instead—thanks for that, Mum and Dad. I wonder if Ellis Joshua Finch would have had a different life to mine. On the day I was born, my Mum donned short bobbed hair after having a breakdown mid-pregnancy and asked her friend to cut all her hair off, regretting this instantly. The family videotapes show her proudly holding me moments after giving birth and that was the point that I met my best friend.

My Mum is the most amazing and complicated woman you could meet, and there is no love like it. My Mum resembles everything about love for me. She loves hard and intensely, and that moment, holding the newborn in her arms, was the start of an amazing relationship. I wish I could go back and tell her now, "We will save each other's lives over and over again. This is the start of our journey together". My Dad with his dark black hair (he no longer has his dark hair) and dark bushy moustache (thankfully he no longer has this either), behind the camera proudly, videoing every slight moment, capturing a moment that we all would laugh over every time we rewatch these videos–the midwife changing me to reveal two very large testicles! Thanks for that, Dad! If I could go back to the moment of meeting my Dad for the first time, I'd say very similar things to my Mum. Still, I'd also say, "Thanks for loving me as much as you are going to, thanks for accepting me for exactly who I'm going to be and forever putting a smile on my face through the hard times that are to come ". If there is one thing my Dad can do, it's put a smile on somebody's face. It may be a very shit Dad joke or from his nervous laugh that I have unfortunately inherited.

My parents are amazing and I'm so lucky to have them. Yes, we've been through some ridiculously hard times together, but I'm forever grateful for them. There are others out there who have lost their parents at an early age, never known their parents, had parents walk away from them, parents who didn't like them, parents who abused them and those who just don't have good relationships with their parents and if you think you can relate to any of those then I hand on heart send my love to you, because without my parents I would not be here right now, so please love yourself that bit more for getting through life without the support I received, because you are stronger than I could ever be.

I'm their third surviving child, their final child. My eldest brother, Adam, was born seven years before me. For most of my childhood, Adam was the moody older brother. He'd sit in his room and I used to just annoy him. We'd have arguments and play fights that got out of hand, and one of us would get hurt, usually me. I remember us play fighting on our parent's bed. He knocked me with a pillow, sending my little body flying and crashing into the corner of the bedside table, resulting in cracking my head open and a trip to A&E. Of course, when I was really young, back before my memory holds, he would have played with me and helped look after me. Still, for the most part of my memory, he was the moody teenager with a long fringe and nothing in common with me. But as we both have matured, we have a great relationship—he's the first to ring my phone when he knows I'm struggling, he's always there with words of wisdom and encouragement and he stood there on the day I got married and was so proud of his little brother. Adam, to me, just resembles the ideal big brother. Connah is only 19 months older than me. My parents definitely didn't plan on having a third child so soon after experiencing Connah as a newborn baby. Connah was a handful. He still is, he's stressful, aggressive and argumentative, but he is also so passionate, protective and powerful. We would always be throwing awful insults at one another growing up, making each other cry, getting angry and frustrated with one another, but the second anyone in school would call me "gay", "faggot" or attempt to hurt me, he was straight there defending me—even hanging one boy's head into a busy main road in order to terrify him into apologising. That was Connah for you. He's extreme, but he's extremely protective of our family and I wouldn't have him any other way.

Before myself and Connah were born, my parents had to go through an awful experience, probably the most awful experience a parent can go through, losing a child. On the 13th January 1990, my sister Chelsey was born with her heart no longer beating. In a nutshell, she was delivered too late, and there was neglect from the professional side. It's something our family has never got over. We were raised with Chelsey very much a part of our lives. Some may not understand why, some may say it's strange. I know some even condemned my parents for having their breathless baby christened before laying her to rest, but what I will say is, wow, she is loved. She is loved by every single one of us, her parents, her brothers, her grandparents and more. It's always been a difficult question for me "Do you have any siblings?" The answer, of course, yes! The follow up is usually "Oh, brothers or sisters?" The answer, "Two brothers and a sister". It's not something I've ever kept hidden, but to then explain "but my sister passed away" is always awkward for the person to hear. However, I will never deny her existence. Chelsey may never have walked this earth, she may never have breathed in this air, but she existed, she is in each of our hearts and she is so loved. You may have said to yourself, you can't wait for the day to be reunited with your loved ones who have passed away, your grandparents, your parents, your relatives, your friends or even horrifically your own children. I, myself, cannot wait to meet my sister. If a clairvoyant I saw a few years ago is to be believed (which I cannot stress enough I do, but I know there are those out there who don't believe or choose not to), then the day I see Chelsey will be not to meet her but to be reunited with her. For any parent who has lost a child the way my parents did, my heart goes out for you. I have seen first-hand what this experience can do to young parents and how it has shaped the rest of their lives. They will never be the same again since losing her. The one thing my Dad has said and I believe this helps him get through each day without her, he was told himself by a clairvoyant some years ago "Chelsey was never meant to walk this earth, she was simply here to brush into their lives and set the path for the rest" and that she certainly did.

Childhood is defined as "the state or period of being a child". It is seen by many as "a happy time" or "the best time" and "it's all downhill from there". These are some statements I heard continuously growing up and questioned. Can I say I had many happy moments as a child? Yes of course! My parents did everything they could to give us the best that they could. We had the best parties, the best cakes, the best presents for our birthdays, at Christmas we each had a space in the living room filled with a tower of presents and we went on some incredible holidays together in Florida, Turkey, North Wales and the rest. Of course, I'm incredibly grateful for those moments, as there are some out there who would do anything to swap their childhood for mine. I can only apologise to those who may see me as ungrateful and unappreciative. I cannot stress that is not what I am. I know how lucky I am to have had these moments with my family and I know the sacrifices my parents made to make those moments happy but sadly when I look back at childhood, it just wasn't a happy time for me. I never felt truly happy. I just felt numb.

From an early age, I remember feeling isolated at school. I wasn't sporty like the other boys, so I didn't fit in there. I wasn't "girly" enough for the girls, and believe me, I even tried there. I was just there, existing. I wasn't in a cliche, nor in a group. I was just simply there. I tried so hard to be like the other boys. I remember one summer before I went into secondary school, my brother, Connah, spending the six week holidays attempting to teach me how to play football, the rules of the game, the skill of the game, the different teams and the main players just so I could have something in common with the other boys in my year. I even made a website (A Piczo one for all the 90s generation who remember) about how much I loved football—the reality was I never really got it. I don't hate it, I just don't enjoy it. Rugby was even worse. I dreaded playing rugby at school. One of my high school PE Teachers made a point of repeatedly calling me "Persil Boy" as my PE Kit came off the pitch just as clean as it went on, I can laugh about it now, but at the time, I felt humiliated and it only fuelled the bullies with more ammunition to throw at me on a daily basis. Standing there in a circle of the classmates, majority covered head-to-toe in mud, sweat dripping off their red cheeks, I stood there, my PE kit still acceptable to wear for the next lesson, my skin just as pale as ever and standing there in a group of 20–30 boys, 2 or 3 teachers and I never felt as lonely.

Majority of my school years, I spent most of my time with the girls. This definitely didn't help with the bullying, again it was more ammunition for them, but I didn't have to worry about being so different from them. Until I was so completely different from them. In primary school, there wasn't much difference between us. We played with soft toys, played make-believe story games, talked about pets and celebrities and spent our time having fun and laughing. I had some great female friends from primary school, some that I still try to keep in contact with now. But as the girls grew older, I would notice differences between us. The first was the phase of Bratz Dolls (again, 90s generation you'll remember). The group of girls I was friends with all had the latest ones. I remember asking my Mum if I could get one for a birthday or Christmas, and her answer was, "You aren't having a Bratz Doll!" We spoke about this recently together and she can't even remember saying that, but that moment for me was when I realised I didn't fit in with the group of girls either. I wasn't allowed a Bratz Doll. The doll was for girls, which would make the bullies only have another reason to bully me more. I was that desperate to fit in. I even stole one girl's doll after she allowed me to play with it. I went to the fancy dress shop in town, purchased some black spray paint for hair, took the doll home and attempted to spray paint the hair black to disguise it as a completely different doll to the one she had allowed me to borrow, just so I could join in the next day with my own doll. Unfortunately, it was pretty obvious what I had done because the paint just stained my hands the next day, luckily she forgave me quite quickly, didn't tell our friends I was the thief and comforted me when I got upset that I wasn't allowed one. Nowadays, that girl is now a he and I'm so unbelievably proud of the man he is today.

The second time I remember feeling very different to this group of girls was our last year in primary school. During the summer holidays that I had spent learning the rules and skills of football with my brother, my friends and I decided to go swimming at the local swimming baths without our parents. I loved swimming (still do now). It's a safe haven for me being under the water. So I was very excited to go swimming with friends. We arrived at the leisure centre, paid our fees and memberships and walked to the changing rooms. That moment as the girls carried on walking down the hallway to the female changing room and I had to turn left for the male changing room, was a moment I felt different to them and standing getting changed on my own, being as quick as possible, so I could be back with my friends again was such a lonely experience.

As I went into secondary school, the bullying only increased. My parents and primary school teachers had tried to prepare me for this and in some ways avoid it from happening even if it meant I wasn't being myself. One primary teacher tried her best to make me bond with the boys in my class, she even asked all the girls to come stand up on the wall overlooking the playground with her so that I had to go join in with the football with the boys for 20 minutes. I walked over, holding back tears in my eyes at how isolated and different I felt to everyone around me. I knew those boys didn't want me to join in and play football with them. They didn't like me and weren't afraid to show it. Once I had done my time playing football with them (I say played, I stood with them waiting for it to be over), the girls were allowed to return to the playground and I was allowed to join in and play with them again. I thank that teacher for trying, but yeah can't say it helped my mental health that day at all. Although I appreciate what she was trying to do. The same teacher tried again to make me build a friendship with the boys in my class earlier in my education. We had a trip to Winmarleigh Hall in Lancashire, where we stayed over for 2 nights and got involved in outdoor activities such as zip-lining, sports day and climbing. I originally refused to go on this school trip, as the boys and girls were to be in separate room accommodation and I knew none of the boys would want to share a room with me, but the teacher got in touch with my Mum and expressed she thought it would be good for me. She put me in a room with three other boys. One was probably the most popular boy in the school year, one of his friends, and the other boy was relatively quiet but accepted by the boys more than I was. The school trip ended up being more fun than I expected, and I actually had a really good time. The boys I shared a room with all got me involved and I even had a good bond with the popular boy over the girls we fancied from our class. But sadly, when we got back to school, everything went back as it was. He was the popular boy, and I was the weird quiet kid who didn't like football and played with the girls. Sorry teacher, mission failed.

It was difficult to go through those young years trying to fit in, not quite sure where. As I'm writing this, more memories come to my head of little moments of primary school. I remember when a new headteacher came along and the name of the school was changed to match the parish church. We were all so angry at the name change—one of the girls said, "We can't just let it happen. The guys on 'Recess' wouldn't put up with this!" (Another throwback for our generation there!) Moments like that put a massive smile on my face now. Did any other school put a buttercup flower underneath your chin to see if you liked butter or not? It worked for me, so I can vouch that this seemed valid at the time. I was a dramatic child and I even once told my friends that I had found out my Dad wasn't my biological Dad and that my biological Dad's name was Jonathon Jackson just because I'd watch the scenario on a film and wanted my own initials to match so I could be nicknamed "JJ". Looking back, this may have been a red flag that I wasn't quite accepting of myself.

Now, I know I've said my parents were amazing. And they were. But they weren't perfect. And neither was their marriage. They had their issues and as their children, we were exposed to it. Some may disagree and say it was wrong for them to argue in front of us, and I can't argue against those that do disagree, but it's reality. Marriages are hard work, something I'm learning myself now. So I did spend a lot of my childhood listening to them arguing. I would sit at the top step of the staircase, listening to my Mum crying and shouting at my Dad, my Dad would shout back, and eventually, he'd go out in his car and I would always worry he wasn't going to come back. He always did and that I'm so grateful for and feel for those who read this and remember when their fathers or mothers didn't come back home. I would console my Mum a lot as a child. Like I said, it was the start of an amazing relationship. We were and still are each other's rocks, and that means it comes with the hard times. There was a time when me and Connah went to stay at my Nan's house overnight due to them falling out. The next day my Mum came to collect us and her eyes told me she hadn't slept or stopped crying. Connah repeatedly asked, "Where's Dad? Is he at home?" from the back seat on the way home. I sat in the passenger seat looking at my Mum, her eyes filled with tears at the thought of her marriage being over. My main concern was, "Mum, calm down, just focus on driving and get us home." I was terrified that she was that emotional and upset that she wouldn't be able to see properly and may even crash the car. I was worried for her and my brother at that moment, rather than if my parents were going to split up.

Maybe it's every family, but our family couldn't have a holiday without there being a fallout. We used to visit Turkey a lot as my Gran, my Dad's Mum, lived there for the majority of the year. She was involved with business over there and would spend most of the year there and we would visit for holidays. The summer holidays were amazing spending time with Gran, one thing I will say though, in 55 degrees celsius she would always make a Hot Pot (others call it Lobbies, or Scouse. It's just a potato pie really)—the heat as you ate was unbelievable. But again, my parents would have their quarrels and I found it always affected me more than it appeared to affect my brothers. I found myself getting involved, begging them to stop, comforting my Mum, trying to find my Dad as he stormed off. This occasion in Turkey, my Gran wasn't very happy with my Mum, she doted on my Dad and saw him as an angel, so of course, my Mum must be the evil witch in her eyes then. She was voicing her dislike for my Mum, saying "behaviour is disgusting!" I had my Mum's back and screamed back to my Gran, "Don't speak about my Mum like that!" from the staircase before storming off to the bedroom that I was sharing with my brother Connah. He was asleep. (To anyone who is offended at me shouting back at my Gran and see it as lack of respect for elders, I apologise, but I will always have my Mum's back!)

There were some amazing times there in Turkey, dancing in the club to the obviously traditional Turkish song "Kiss Kiss" (sarcasm there), going to the water parks, I used to climb all the way to the top of the black hole slide with my Dad and then bottle it coming back down the steps on my own, meaning my Dad had to take the rubber dingy and go down the slide solo, probably looking a little creepy to all the parents waiting for their children at the bottom. There were also jeep safaris to the local villages and meeting families from the village. I found this experience amazing. My Gran had a business partner who we spent a lot of our time with, including his wife and daughter. His daughter didn't speak any English at the time but somehow the two of us managed to find a way to communicate with one another in order for us to play together in the pool and the parks. One thing I will say about having those experiences of going to Turkey from such a young age, I have never ever understood why anybody can be racist. I loved everybody we met in Turkey, the staff who worked for my

Gran and her business partner and other guests. They all adored us and treated us like family. I know some will be rolling their eyes saying it was to get a tip or they have a view that "all Turkish men are con artists trying to get a visa", but that just wasn't the case, The Finch Family had a special place in their hearts and they did ours. So I'm so grateful for my Gran and my parents for allowing us to have these experiences.

Another moment from childhood we all laugh about now—well, everyone except my Mum. We went on an amazing holiday to Florida. It must have cost my parents a fortune to get us there and they sacrificed a lot—which more than likely added a lot of stress to their marriage leading up to this. One day we were walking around 'Universal Studios', I can't remember why they fell out, I just know they did and my Mum didn't want to speak to any of us that day. On the ride 'Earthquake' (which is no longer there) going underground on a train an earthquake happens and, you have water flowing in and cars falling into the train, it's all exciting and entertaining—my Mum sat arms tightly folded, fuming face on in full force being jolted around by the train without breaking out her composure or facial expression. Leaving the ride, Mum stormed off and went missing for a little while. We continued going on rides with Dad whilst trying to find Mum at the same time. Eventually, I spotted her across the lake as she sat smoking a cigarette on a picnic bench by herself. I shouted over, "Mum! Mum!" waving across the lake to her, she took one look over, spotted my Dad and flipped him the bird. The holiday to Florida was amazing, and the last holiday we had as a full family. We did everything there was to do, all the theme parks, the water parks, the tourist attractions, the beaches and even swimming with dolphins at 'Discovery Cove'. It was brilliant to watch my Mum finally experience her dream and swim with a dolphin and watch the firework display at Magic Kingdom. Although she was devastated, we never got to see Tinker-Bell fly down due to the potential thunderstorm and bad weather. We actually almost emigrated to Florida in 2006. My parents returned shortly after our family holiday to begin looking at property, schools and businesses. I couldn't wait at the time. I felt like I belonged there. The music and the entertainment industry was more respected there. Maybe I wouldn't get bullied for enjoying singing and dancing there. However, due to the start of the recession in England, making it a struggle to sell our family home and then my brother, Adam, starting a relationship, it sadly wasn't meant to be, and we remained in England.

We once went to Center Parcs with my Auntie, Uncle, a cousin I was very close to and her new baby brother. One evening, Connah had taken a play fight too far and made me cry, which wasn't exactly a shock or difficult to do—I was really sensitive and cried a lot. After drinking too much, my Dad punished Connah too harshly and my Mum went in to intervene, defend Connah and stop the shouting. It turned into my parents arguing instead, Dad storming out of the cabin into the dark, into the woods, not knowing if he was coming back again. My Mum packed our suitcases quicker than if the apocalypse was happening and planned to cut the holiday short. Fortunately, we didn't. The next day, the hungover adults sorted their quarrels out, and we had a great rest of the holiday riding bikes through the woods, swimming at the local swimming centre and playing badminton, all together. I was very close to my cousin around this time. We were inseparable. We spent a lot of our time together. I felt I fitted in with her more than most people. We used to sing, dance, and play make-believe games. Pretending to be celebrities in these games, I would always pretend to be Britney Spears. She was a role model in my life at the time. I loved her music, her look and everything about her. She was the first CD I ever bought. I wanted to be Britney Spears and everything she was and I didn't understand then that being male that I couldn't. I had a folder of all different images of her that I would carry around with me, taking into school to show my friends and even on the occasion when I dramatically ran away from home, I didn't take food, clothes or money, I took the main essential item, and that was my Britney Spears folder. My innocence said, "I want to pretend to be her in this game I'm playing with my cousin", but now looking back and learning what I know about myself now, this was a massive red flag that I wasn't happy or comfortable as myself and felt more comfortable when I would pretend to be someone else, someone that just oozed confidence. Around this time, I started to sing a lot. We had a second living room in our home, so that room was mainly used by myself and my Dad to sing on the karaoke machine. I loved to sing. It was escapism. I loved the way it made me feel, how I felt like somebody else and would envision being on a stage singing for thousands of people just like Britney Spears did. According to those who got to hear me sing, I was quite good. Of course, this was before puberty and I once could reach those higher notes. Once everyone was singing karaoke at a family gathering and I started to sing 'I'm Not A Girl, Not Yet A Woman', this was being completely naive to the meaning of the lyrics. I just wanted to sing a nice song. My Nan, my Mum's Mum, turned to my Mum as I sang and asked, "What's he singing this for?" During a hypnotherapy master class recently, this was a moment that I pinpointed as the moment my confidence was first negatively affected. I hid away upstairs in my bedroom, feeling embarrassed and upset, luckily my Nan realised her comment had upset me and came upstairs to apologise and explain she didn't care what I sang but thought I could sing better songs, explaining she wasn't really a Britney Spears fan. I didn't believe her, and I won't ever know if that was the real reason or not, but it never stopped me singing Britney Spears again, but I would carefully select which songs I would sing publicly or not. Britney Spears went on to have her issues publicly, that I fearfully watched unfold on the news at a time I was struggling with my own mental health.

CHAPTER TWO

Going into high school was the time that my mental health issues started to become quite evident. The first day is always the most nerve-wracking. I tried to do my primary teacher proud and spent more time with the boys from my class, but one boy started laughing about how I had cried with the girls on the last day of primary school. I knew then that I was never going to be one of them and they wouldn't accept me as one of them either.

It was during the first year of high school I realised that being a Britney Spears fan and listening to pop music wasn't classed as "cool" and started to hide this side of me to most people other than my close friends. I used to speak quite well and was even nicknamed by my family as "Poshy Joshy". However, when I started high school, the boys started to mimic how I spoke and say I sounded "gay". I put on a more broad Wigan accent in order to fit in and the accent stuck over time. Our school had a trend going around that having a combover to the left made you "gay", so of course, the fact my combover did that must mean I was "gay" to them. The fact is, combovers have nothing to do with sexuality. They are best styled when they follow the natural hair growth pattern, something I learnt years later during my training of becoming a barber. The generation I was in at school, I think, was the bridge between being either condemned for being gay or being accepted for being gay. Being gay was still taboo, 'strange', 'abnormal' or even 'weird', but some boys and some girls came out as either gay and bisexual and would be proud of their difference. During this time, I didn't believe I was gay. I actually was really confused why everyone seemed to think I was. Maybe I did know but had suppressed it instead of addressing it.

I did have relationships in high school, well, friendships where sometimes we might have kissed. I was really close friends with the girls, so I found that because I knew what they liked and didn't like from the boys, I could become the "perfect boyfriend" image that they seem to desire, but most girls wanted the class clown or the football captain, not the shy quiet lad who didn't like sport.

The bullying became a lot more intense at high school. It started off with name-calling but soon became physical violence. One day, I walked down a school corridor with two of my female friends when a Year 11 male student pushed me to the floor before picking me up and carrying me away from my two friends. He and his friends slammed me into the lockers and continuously shouted in my face, "Admit you are gay!" I refused. Eventually, he dropped me to the floor and walked away with his friends laughing. I was embarrassed and humiliated and when I got back to my friends, I just told them they had pushed me around and hurt my arm. I went home and told my Mum in a flood of tears and showed her the bruises on my back and on the back of my arms. The next day, it was reported to the school, who did what they could and punished the Year 11 with detention. Although he was punished, it only got worse after that. Not long after the incident, he followed me on the way home from school as I walked home with my friends. He caught up with me and mockingly asked, "You okay Joshy?" I smiled uncomfortably and told him, "I'm fine". My friends were all going silent and feeling awkward, his friends all laughing and waiting for him to act. As a bus was coming along carrying pupils from the school the boy pushed me into the road and I was almost hit by the bus. Luckily, I only had a bruised shoulder from hitting the road. The bus driver wasn't going very fast, so fortunately managed to stop before hitting me. The driver reported the incident to the school. I wasn't at the meeting but I remember afterwards my Mum was furious at the school as they suggested the best thing to do was for me to switch schools instead of tackling the situation. I refused and told my Mum, "I'm going to get bullied anywhere I go, so what is the point?" The Year 11 boy was suspended from school before his exams.

Another boy from my own school year picked up where the bully left off and continued calling me "gay boy", etc, on a daily basis. There was a time I had been shopping in Wigan with my friends and on the bus ride home, this boy and his friends were on the back of the bus shouting down the bus to me asking, "Have you just bought a dress?" I got off on my own at the stop closest to my estate. As I walked across the field, I noticed they had gotten off too. I knew they didn't live near me, so I became worried that they were following me. I ran home and locked the door after realising nobody else was home. They started to knock on the front door and shout horrible names through the letterbox. When that didn't give them a reaction, they started to throw stones at the windows and threatened to burn the house down with me inside and I started to panic that they would break-in and come hurt me. That was the very first time I had a full-blown panic attack where I thought I was going to die. Luckily, my Mum returned home with my brother Connah. The main culprit of the group shouted something horrible to my Mum, making Connah run like an athlete after him. He chased them across the field and then pushed him to the floor before hanging him over the main road until he apologised to me and even stuffing him into a bin. The next day in the canteen at school, this boy forcefully apologised and instead kept quiet as his friends continued the bullying. This boy apologised sincerely to me at the age of eighteen for making my life hell and I accepted his apology. I wish I could say I forgave and forgot, but anyone who is reading and also got bullied as a child will understand. You don't forget. You don't forget the names they called you, the way they mimicked your voice and the way they hurt you.

Unfortunately, the bullying wasn't exclusive to just my time in school. Sometimes the other kids who lived on the street would make comments about me. I was once playing with a basketball by myself in the back garden and the ball went over the gate to the front of the house. I went to get the ball and as I walked back I heard one boy say "Look how he walks" another shouted, "Oi Faggot! Why do you walk like a girl?". I got so upset to my brother Adam, who then told my Mum. My Mum was furious so she went around to this boy's house and informed his Mum how her son was making me feel. An hour or so later, the boy's Mum and he came around to apologise. I awkwardly said, "it's okay", but just so everyone is clear and knows, it wasn't okay. It just wasn't okay. Bullying someone and then apologising to them expecting them to be completely ok, is like screwing up a piece of paper, unfolding it and expecting it to be exactly how it once was. It won't be. The paper will always have those creases and signs of damage visible and so do the victims of bullying, they will carry the words and traumatic memories with them forever.

I would love to turn around here and say I had lots of happy memories of high school, but the reality was, I absolutely hated going. I pretended to be ill so many times just so my Mum wouldn't send me in. If that didn't work and she did send me in, I would pretend to be ill to the teachers, so they would ask her to come to collect me instead. I would make myself vomit so that I would look ill and there would be evidence I was feeling unwell. I would purposely leave my PE kit at home and say I forgot it. One time I even stuffed my PE bag behind one of the bins at the back of the school, so if they checked my locker it wasn't there. The PE teachers took an instant disliking to me and all my attempts to get out of taking part and sometimes they would mock me in the changing rooms in front of all the other boys in my year. The worst was thinking I'd get away with not taking part for forgetting my kit, but they'd tell me to go to the cupboard and get the lost and found kit, which was a smelly old used kit that had been left behind, didn't fit properly and most likely never washed each time it was worn—more humiliation. I once pretended I had to leave the lesson early for a dentist appointment, but with no note, the teacher refused to let me leave and joined in as the other boys laughed at my attempt to not play sports. I did enjoy basketball, cross country and badminton, but that was about it and it wasn't enough for the teachers or the other boys.

At around the age of 13, I began to self-harm. I can't remember the first time why and what happened, but it became a regular thing. It didn't start off dangerous; I would use a sharp wire to just scratch the surface of the skin, and the burning sensation would be enough to distract my mind from what I was thinking and to focus on the pain. I remember walking to my friend's house after hurting myself, and the feel of the sting as the cold air and the wind hit the scratches felt so satisfying. I was punishing myself for things that were completely out of my control, but I hated myself anyway. I felt like I deserved to feel this way because of how I was. It was my own fault. Eventually, I opened up to a close friend who told another friend, and that friend told her parents. Her parents contacted the school with their concerns. My form teacher was informed, and she spoke with my parents at a parent's evening. I remember Mum coming home holding back tears, and I thought I was in serious trouble. Both my brothers went to this high school before me, and both were continuously getting bad reports on parents evening. It was normal for 'the serious chat' after a parents evening. However, most of my parents' evenings reports had been "he's too quiet and shy, he needs to get involved more". The worst being "he needs to stop talking to his friends during lessons". But this time, I could tell something was bothering my Mum, she cried a lot telling me what my form teacher had informed them and I cried back telling them how the bullying had gotten worse, and I didn't want to go to school anymore. The school assigned me a school therapist, and a comment was made to my Mum by my head-of-year that this "could just be attention-seeking behaviour". Amazing support (sarcasm). The school therapist was okay but didn't seem to understand me. She would continuously tell me, "you are young, you should be filled with happiness". But at that age and how I felt, I didn't know of happiness. I'd never felt happy before. My Mum wasn't very impressed with the school's help and took me to the doctors herself, then referred me to Child and Adolescent Mental Health Services (CAMS), and I started to have weekly counselling sessions with my parents present. The therapist would repeatedly ask to see me without my parents, but I didn't feel confident enough without them. I can't tell you exactly how it went down, but I stopped the sessions, and my Mum became irritated that they seemed to be trying to blame my parents for how I felt instead of addressing the issues. So I continued to see the school's therapist and also the School's Chaplin, who would suggest drawing pictures of things that made me happy in a journal. I can't say that ever worked or made me feel any better, but I do massively appreciate the help and support the school, the school counsellor, the school Chaplin, and the CAMS team showed me. I just think it was a bigger issue than they even realised. You have to remember, this was a time before people spoke about mental health issues. It was a time where Britney Spears was being called "crazy" instead of people having sympathy for her. There wasn't a chance I was telling anyone that at the age of 13 years old, I had been diagnosed with depression and severe anxiety.

    My only escapism at this time was singing and dancing. I was smart enough to know that this could never be public knowledge, so it all stayed within our family home. Until a family holiday to 'Flamingo Land'. There was a talent show at the local clubhouse, and my parents encouraged me to take part. I felt too shy and nervous to try, so I refused and carried on the day as normal, going on the rides and looking at the animals in the zoo. We went to the clubhouse in the evening and watched these other kids get up to sing, dance, act, juggle. I turned to my Mum and said, "I want to do it". I knew nobody knew me here, so what was the worst that could happen? My Dad went up to the show host and asked if I could sing. The host told him I couldn't take part in the talent show as entries had closed, but I could get up and sing if I wanted to. I got up and sang acapella and I got a standing ovation from the crowd. I loved being applauded and the feeling it gave me. I ran back to my seat and hugged my Mum. The host came over and told my Dad, "When we call the other children up, Josh needs to come on stage too," so I did as they said, joining the other kids on stage. I'd like to say I didn't know what was happening and it was all a surprise, but as I climbed the steps to the stage, I spotted a certificate with my name on it to say I had won the talent show. I did my best to act surprised and smiled as I accepted the certificate. I actually cried once we left the club. I think it was a relief. I thought I'd found somewhere to fit in and be accepted. I wanted to feel like this all the time. I wanted to sing. We were invited back to sing at the finals and enjoy a free holiday weekend. My cousin also joined us. When we returned, we practically had the theme park to ourselves as it was during school term so we could go round the rides over and over again. At the dress rehearsal in the afternoon, I was really nervous and almost decided to not do the final. My Mum said, "if you don't want to do it, don't do it, we've got a holiday out of this anyway!" But I went through with it. I sang on stage. I pulled that microphone out of the stand and sang my little heart out. But it wasn't enough, I didn't win, I lost to a really young boy who tap-danced, but I won myself that night because as I got off the stage after singing, both my Mum and my Dad stood there crying with proudness.

  I went on and auditioned for the BBC television show 'I'd Do Anything' to compete for the role of Oliver Twist in the West End. I remember sitting in the hall waiting to be called in, watching all these confident children practising their lines and their singing, some singing in cockney accents. I'd just gone completely as myself with my Mum and Dad, no experience of drama school. My drama teacher at school had recommended this audition to two other boys and me, but only I ended up there. I hoped to make her proud. My name was called into a group and off we went to a separate room to do our audition. Four of us had to line up at a time and sing a few lines each, but they wanted us to play the role of The Artful Dodger as we sang. This wasn't something I had expected, and singing in an accent wasn't something I had ever done before. I knew as soon as I finished singing the producer wasn't very impressed, so I had already given hope. There were around 20–30 boys in the room, and only two names were given a call back, they just so happened to be two identical twins. The producer claimed to have no idea.

It was one thing taking part in a talent show away from where we lived and doing an audition for a role I knew I wouldn't get, but I decided I wanted to audition for "Britain's Got Talent". I had just taken part in a children's confidence-building course recommended by my Dad. At the end of the course, I decided I wanted to audition and hopefully get somewhere with my singing. I can't remember how, but the local newspaper got wind that I was one of the first children to pass the course I attended and that I was auditioning for 'Britain's Got Talent'. They came around the house and took photographs of me smiling and holding a microphone. I remember him asking me repeatedly to "drop your shoulders". I didn't realise that I had been permanently holding my shoulders up due to how tense and on-edge I felt. Until that point, I never realised how I felt was starting to show on the outside too. The newspaper was published. I didn't know when until another pupil messaged me on MSN (throwback!) to tell me she had seen me in the paper. The next day, the Headteacher spotted me in the corridor and pulled me aside to wish me luck in my audition. I felt like this could potentially make me cool. Maybe people would see it as I might be famous one day and want to be my friend. But no, the picture of me in the newspaper was brought into school and passed around. One was placed in my form room with the words "gay boy" written over it. My confidence was shattered. I still went ahead with the audition. It was back when the judges were Simon Cowell, Amanda Holden and Piers Morgan. It was quite a relatively new programme then, so the budget wasn't as high as it is today.

The original audition was just in a hotel in Manchester. I went with my Mum and my Dad and was called back for a second audition which was in a bigger hotel. I sang Maroon 5 "She Will Be Loved" with a camera and extremely bright lights in my face and felt the nerves taking over. Sadly I didn't get through this audition (which confused me at the time as all the comedy acts / "the rubbish ones" were getting through the first audition and then this stage too), but they kindly advised me to come back in another year when I was a bit older and more confident. I am so thankful that no footage filmed ever made it to YouTube or TV. I knew after the newspaper incident it would just be laughed at by the whole school. Unfortunately, not getting through the audition wasn't the only bad experience for me that week. Our family changed the night of my audition and it wasn't for the better.

 We'd got home from the failed audition, and I got straight in bed, ready for school in the morning. When I got up that morning, my Mum and Dad's beds were empty. My brother, Adam, explained that our Gran had collapsed in the night and been taken to hospital. I didn't really panic. Gran had been diagnosed with swine flu a few weeks previously. It was during the time that swine flu was all over the TV and newspapers, but I wasn't worried about her—Gran was a healthy 68-year-old woman. She didn't smoke and hadn't drank in years and spent a lot of her time abroad in the sun. She was getting over her illness, telling my parents the day before that she felt a lot better and to let her know how I got on with the audition. I went into school as normal and remembered sitting in my history class, looking at the clock at 2.15 pm and feeling this intense feeling of dread. Something wasn't right and I wanted to get home. When I got home and Mum and Dad still weren't there, me and Connah started to panic. Eventually, they returned home and sat us down to tell us the doctors did everything they could all day to save her, but our Gran had sadly passed away. I cried a lot. Gran used to love watching me sing and dance. Whenever she visited, she'd ask me to sing and dance for her. I was doing my audition when she collapsed and she never woke up again. I blamed myself for this. I can't remember very much of her funeral other than it was really cold and I couldn't get the courage to carry her coffin with my brothers and cousins. I wish I had spent more time with my Gran. I wish that I had taken more pictures with her. I wish I had rang her more and visited her more because she was an amazing Gran. She loved her sons and her grandchildren so much and we loved her. Ever since she left us, whenever I sing, whenever I have danced, I would always picture my Gran being sat there watching, smiling and clapping. There have been times in the room at home as I was dancing, I would swear I caught a glimpse of her sitting there, I would panic in fear and run to my Mum and Dad, but somehow I knew already that she would be there watching me. I never tried to pursue a singing career after her death, though.

The year after losing my Gran, our family suffered another great loss. This time it was our Grandad Tommy, my Mum's Dad. He was diagnosed with multi neurone disease after what they originally thought to be a stroke. Grandad Tommy was a very proud man, the idea of being dependent on his family wasn't right for him, he asked to be taken to Switzerland so he could leave us of his choice and not the disease taking him and his dignity, but it wasn't something any family member could do easily. Before he passed, he lost his mobility, his voice and an incredible amount of weight. I remember when he was still able to walk, he slowly walked into the living room. He looked so thin, he reminded me of the photographs and videos of the victims of the concentration camps from the Second World War. My Nan and Grandad had a peculiar and funny relationship, they would pretend they no longer loved each other, and she would shout and say, "I'll dance on your grave one day", but when Grandad left us, he took more than half of my Nan with him. She was never the same woman again, and a year later, she suffered a heart attack. During the operation her heart stopped and she had to be resuscitated but then during an X-Ray, cancer was found on her lungs.

In my last year of high school, I started to self-harm more severely. In some phases, it was becoming an everyday occurrence. This was the start of the addiction happening. It became such a norm in our household that my brother Connah shouted at me once for getting blood on his recently washed trainers that were drying on the radiator in the bathroom. The issue wasn't that I had self-harmed to the point of bleeding. It was that I had ruined his trainers. This wasn't his fault, or in any way am I blaming him for it—it had just become pretty standard for us. My family did everything they could to make me feel loved, to stop me from doing this to myself and protect me, but even when they took anything I could use away from me, I would use my own nails to scratch myself repeatedly. The need to self-harm became much stronger, but just scratching the surface of the skin was no longer fulfilling the urge and I began to cut deeper and more frequently leaving scars on my forearms and wrist. I remember one cut being so severe that it bled excessively and I panicked it wasn't going to stop, I grabbed some towels and eventually got it to stop and it healed with a large scab over it.

My Mum spotted this scab when we visited a family friend's house and took me back to the doctors the next day. Unfortunately, I had lost my faith in doctors by this point. Up until very recently, I hadn't addressed this. I had suppressed this memory for over ten years until the point I had practically removed it from my conscious memory.

CHAPTER THREE

I was having a bath one night when I found a lump in one of my testicles. Of course, instantly, I began to panic, and my mind went straight to worrying that I may have testicular cancer. I examined and examined this lump, driving myself mad with theories of cancer and worries that I would have to have my testicle removed or undergo chemotherapy. I decided to speak to my Mum straight away about this, although it's always an awkward one getting your balls out for your Mum to check, but she was my Mum and also worked at the hospital, so it made sense to confide in her with my worry. Needs must. My Mum insisted that I go to our GP Practice and have this seen by the doctor. I remember going to see our family doctor, and feeling awkward and nervous about the idea of having to get my private parts out, what the outcome may be and being completely honest I was also really worried that if the doctor was examining my testicles and feeling them, that I may end up with an unwanted erection (as a young teen, it didn't exactly take much to—sorry, Mum and Dad). The doctor at the GP surgery was really good and professional about it all. Although he had a student doctor with him, the examination was quick and assertive. He reassured me he wasn't overly concerned with the lump being cancerous, he referred me to have an ultrasound scan done at the local hospital in order to be completely sure what the lump was and deal with whatever it was once we knew more about it.

If I remember correctly, the ultrasound scan was a couple of months later. I got a letter to explain that I would be having it done at the hospital where my Mum worked. I don't remember who I went with to the appointment or even who took me there (until recently, I had removed all this knowledge and information from my conscious memory). I attended my appointment for the ultrasound. I remember it being quite a dark room as I walked in, the computer screen on the left of the room and the bed across to the left. The doctor was a really large, black, bald male and I remember thinking he was so big that the swivel chair looked bizarrely small underneath him and I was surprised it didn't break. He was really quiet greeting me and I noticed that there was nobody else with him, unlike at the GP surgery where the doctor was assisted by a student, but I wasn't concerned about it or uncomfortable with it. I lay down on the bed, pulling my pants down to my thighs and covering my penis with my t-shirt. I got nervous again that an awkward unwanted erection may come about with the examination, so I placed the t-shirt to cover it in case it did. The ultrasound gel was extremely cold and straight away I forgot all about my nerves about how awkward I felt and my thoughts focused on the nerves of what the results of the scan may be. The probe was moved around for a few minutes as the doctor watched the image on the computer screen. I kept my eyes still, staring up at the ceiling. After a few minutes, it felt longer, but I'm sure it was only a few minutes. The doctor began to examine my testicles and the lump. At first I assumed that he must not have been able to find the lump with the probe, or maybe he was just examining it. This continued for a little while and then the doctor began to examine both my testicles, but his movement had changed from just applying pressure to feel for the lump to caressing them. I looked down at him at that point and could see that he was observing them with his head tilted to one side. His facial expression didn't look as though it was medically examining them. He did not look back at me. I returned my eyes back to the ceiling without looking at him again. He used his other hand and pulled my t-shirt up to reveal my penis that was flaccid and he began to caress and feel, not in a professional way. His movement changed then to masturbating my penis (being completely open and honest, it had changed from being flaccid to slightly swollen with the movement, but I never developed a full erection or enjoyed this experience). The doctor then spoke to me for the first time in a while and asked, "Does that feel nice?" He spoke with a slight whisper and an extremely deep voice with an accent I couldn't place. The interruption of silence made me jump, but I didn't move my eyes from the ceiling. I didn't answer his question; I just kept my eyes straight ahead on the ceiling, waiting for it to be over. He continued masturbating and caressing until finally, he stopped. I think maybe he realised that I wasn't enjoying the moment because I didn't have an erection. He let go of me and moved away, returning to looking at the computer screen with his back to me. He told me when I could expect my results, and that was it. He never turned to look back at me. I left the room and as a young teen, I was a little obnoxious in believing that I'd just had my first sexual experience, but I think deep down, I knew what had happened to me was wrong. I didn't tell whoever had taken me to the appointment, nor did I tell anyone again until the age of 25 years old. I think I just wanted to forget all about it, forget that it had happened to me and just move on with my life. Part of me was scared that if anybody found out about this, maybe the bullies would find out and it would only make them call me "gay" and "queer" even more. Nobody would believe I didn't want the doctor to touch me, so it was easier to just deny to myself it ever happened. I questioned myself whether I wanted it to or not. I never told him to stop, I never got off the bed and ran out the room, I never pushed his hands away, I just lay there, frozen.

It's been extremely difficult to talk about this, but I have found the more I've spoken about it, the more I'm accepting moving on. I have learnt through having intense therapy discussions and conversations with others on this that suppressing a traumatic memory may remove the memory, but it doesn't remove the consequences of the event. Even though I decided I no longer wanted to remember what had happened, this is definitely a moment that changed the way I was and the way I am today.

Over the years, there have been a lot of consequences to both the memory and suppressing it for so long. Ever since this I have always asked my Mum to come to any doctor's appointments with me and I've avoided hospital scenarios as much as I can. The memory has sometimes come forward slightly, but never to the point that I would acknowledge its existence. The biggest consequences to it were I relapsed in my addiction to self-harm and at the age of 15 years old, I planned an attempt to end my own life for the first time. Our house was empty one afternoon, so I would be able to do what I needed to do. My plan was that I was going to hang myself from the stair bannister, timed perfectly for when my Mum left work so by the time anyone came home, it would be too late for me to be saved. Everything was going to plan.

After my Mum left for work, I got the rope from my dressing gown, tied it around the stair bannister, and made a loop big enough to get over my head. Jasper, our family dog, started scratching and crying at the kitchen door that led to the hallway where I was. I went down to see what was bothering him and as soon as I opened the kitchen door, he desperately pushed straight past me and went and sat stubbornly on the stairs. I did everything I could to get him back in the kitchen. I opened the back door for him to go outside for a wee, offered him a lot of treats and chew sticks and even tried to pick him up, but failed as he would growl at me. He just wouldn't budge. I decided to sit in the living room for a bit, hoping that he would become curious as to where I was and leave his position on the stairs, giving me time to lock him back in the kitchen, but he never moved. Each time I went to check on him, he was just lying down on the exact same step, not moving. I tried desperately to get him to move as time went on, but he became really aggressive and would bite me with every attempt. However, the second my Mum's car pulled onto the driveway, he jumped down off the stairs and ran into the living room and watched her walk down the drive from the windowsill, wagging his tail with happiness. I only had seconds to run upstairs and hide the evidence of what I had planned to do that day. Now, to some people, it may seem just a coincidence. To others, it doesn't make any sense, but to me, I know that Jasper knew what was happening inside my head. I think he could sense how low I was feeling and I truly believe someone up there did everything they could to delay what I was planning to do until it was too late and my plan had failed.

Around the time of the incident with the doctor, I was already having some counselling sessions. I remember being given some advice about what to do when struggling to deal with certain situations. The advice was to create a character in your head and give them my problems, so I did just that. I created the character, Elle. Elle was a young blonde female pop star who had become successful at a young age. She could deal with this for me instead, this all could have happened to her at a young age and so she used it as motivation to achieve her dreams. I spent so much time envisioning this character as a real person that it confused myself at times and I questioned if I wanted to be her instead. I now know that the therapist who gave the advice should have also advised on how to let go of the character when they are no longer necessary. For a short period of time, I became worried if I may have been showing signs of schizophrenia. I know now through sessions with my current therapist that the character was created as a defence mechanism in order to protect myself from situations that gave me anxiety and could cause me emotional harm. This is when the character would step in. I would envision myself as her instead and deal with the situation with a more confident persona. Being the negative mindset that I was in, I became worried that the character being there in my mind meant that I would one day inevitably become a transgender woman, but deep down, I knew this wasn't what I wanted, nor who I am. I will say after questioning myself for that period of time, I have such huge respect for anyone who is transgender as it must be such a confusing experience for them to grow up in and then to have the courage to be themselves in the scary society of today is amazing, and they deserve every ounce of respect that anyone can give them.

There were consequences to my behaviour from suppressing the memory too. In 2018, I ended up in hospital with unbearable pain in the back of my head. They suspected a possible bleed on the brain, so they sent me down to have two CT scans. They came back to say they wanted to perform a lumbar puncture into my spine to completely rule out an ongoing bleed. I had been worried this would be the outcome as both my brother and friend had suffered one, and both explained the suffering of having it done—it's not exactly pleasant. The doctor apologised that there was nobody available that day and that they were going to have to keep me overnight and perform the procedure the following day. That was just not an option for me. There was no way I was going to stay overnight on my own. At the time, I didn't realise why, but I was terrified at the idea of being left here alone, so I refused and demanded that if they couldn't do the procedure that day, then I had to discharge myself and leave. I explained to them all that it was just because I didn't want to let my customers down and cancel another day of appointments, but I think I was panicking out of fear and acting recklessly. Luckily, a doctor was convinced to sacrifice his day off work to come in and perform the lumbar puncture and it was done on the same day with no further bleeding on the brain found. Meaning after two hours of laying completely still,

I could return home and was advised not to return to work the next day—I did.

More recently, I found another lump, but this time it was in my stomach. I had just had a tattoo of a branch of leaves on my ribs, so I was being sensitive when washing in the area whilst in the bath and I felt a small lump deep down. After months of being put off with the doctors, the doctor insisted I was being paranoid and suggested it was skin trauma due to my recent tattoo or it "may have been there for years" (I knew it had not), another ultrasound was done at another hospital (my Mum accompanied me this time and this ultrasound was done by two really lovely medical professionals) and the results were it was an infected lymph node. I suspect this was from stupidly having done tanning injections for a holiday the previous year. The infection got increasingly worse until eventually the lump was pushing outside of my stomach and bruising my skin. On the day of a consultation appointment at a private hospital, the lump painfully burst. The doctor explained that I would have to have the remaining infection removed and said I would be awake for the procedure, meaning I wouldn't have to stay overnight—this seemed perfect to me. The thought of the procedure didn't even scare or worry me at the time. I walked into the hospital (with my Mum) and didn't really feel frightened at all. It was only after being taken down to prepare for the surgery as I waited on the hospital bed that the panic began. The memory of the doctor from all those years ago slightly resurfaced and I experienced another panic attack. The nurses must have assumed I was just worried about having the procedure done. I convinced myself later that it was just that, but I do remember having the fear that all the doctors and nurses were going to inject me with something that would paralyse me and they would all rape me in the surgery room, and nobody would believe me. The operation itself was an awful experience—the anaesthetic was not very successful, meaning that the procedure was extremely painful. Afterwards, I focused more on how bad the experience of surgery was than how bad I had panicked before going into theatre.

Over ten years after that first ultrasound, I was having a conversation with a friend who told me she had had a conversation with someone. This person had always struggled with mental health, and I have always felt like I related to them and understood this person as an individual, I felt like I understood them when others didn't. I'm not going to go into too much detail because that is their story and their own conversation to have, but this person had also been touched inappropriately by a medical professional at a young age. As my friend confided in me what her own friend had gone through, I felt the memory of my own experience make its way forward and take place in my conscious mind. For the first time, I openly admitted not just to my friend but to myself what had happened to me that day over ten years ago. Later the same day, I briefly confided in two of my closest friends and work colleagues, Laura and Claire, but I tried to not make a big deal out of the confession to test how I felt talking about it. All three of my friends that I spoke to that day were so supportive and encouraged me to speak to my therapist about it, as they knew I had already booked an appointment for the following day. Speaking to my therapist was only the third time I was talking about it. It felt like I had kept it inside and bottled up for so long that once I had said the words and told the story once, I just wanted to keep saying it and saying it until I had said it that much that it removed how I felt about it. Sadly, it did not happen that way. From the first day of admittance, I felt my mood completely deteriorate, and I struggled with coming to terms with the idea that I had been sexually molested as a child. Even hearing my therapist say the words "assault" and "molester" felt alien to the situation, as I hadn't adjusted to viewing what happened to me in that way. After therapy, I decided to speak to my husband about what we had discussed in the session that day, as it didn't feel right to admit this to myself, to my friends and to my therapist, but not to him. He is always amazing at handling my mental health issues (which will be discussed later in my story). After a few times of trying to start the conversation and then finding it too difficult and walking away, I sat in the upstairs bathroom running the bath and finally I told him and got really upset.

 I put my head over his shoulder as he hugged me as I couldn't look him in the eye. His response wasn't what I expected. I'm not sure what I expected, to be honest, maybe I expected more anger, more hurt or more frustration, but after I had finished speaking, he thanked me for telling him and comforted me as I was upset. I wondered if he was upset with me for not telling him all this time? Did he not understand suppression? Did he not believe me? I sat down in the bath after he'd gone back downstairs and went over every slight worry, wondering if he was angry with me. We had a conversation over text message, and he explained to me that he wasn't angry with me in any way. He was really angry with the doctor that had done this to me and was trying his best to stay calm and not react because he didn't think I needed that at the moment. Sometimes I think he knows me better than I know myself.

 The next step I made was speaking to my parents about this. Although my husband discouraged me from speaking about it too much (he was worried I was speaking to people about it for their sake and not my own), I felt like my parents had a right to know that this had happened to me. My main concern was if they would agree to leave the situation alone until I was ready or wanted to do anything with it. I knew they were going to be angry and hurt. Especially my Mum. My Dad was collecting me from dropping my car off to be serviced and it was about a 25 minutes drive away from Wigan. I decided it was probably easier to talk to him as he drove, so he was concentrating on driving and wouldn't be able to lose control of his emotions. He really handled hearing what happened brilliantly. He did express he would rather we take further action and have the doctor punished for what he had done to me, but understood that I wasn't ready for that yet and how emotionally challenging going down that route would be for me. My question to him was, "Can Mum handle this?" What you have to understand is that my Mum had suffered a nervous breakdown two years previous and her mental health has been unstable ever since. I didn't want to destroy any progress that she had made in getting stronger or for her to blame herself for what had happened to me. However Dad encouraged me to speak to my Mum. He knows her best and knew that if she found out I didn't tell her to protect her, that would only make her feel more guilty and much worse than she would feel by telling her the same day I told him. As we pulled onto the driveway of their house, I could feel my eyes filling with tears. I had that feeling in the pit of my stomach called dread as my brain shifted through every possible outcome of the upcoming conversation with my Mum. What if she was angry with me? What if she ignores my request to not take further action? What if she rings the GP surgery and asks for my medical history to find out more information? What if this tips her over the edge and results in another mental breakdown for her? Would my brothers and Dad blame me for putting too much stress on her?

 I started to cry the moment the words were coming out of my mouth as I spoke to her about it, and I could see the worry and panic in her eyes as she listened. Her first words were, "You better be joking me!" I panicked that she was angry with me, but then she started to get upset too. She was angry with what had happened to me, not me. I cried a lot during the conversation; I explained how everything that has happened since this horrible memory now makes sense and how hurt I am dealing with it now rather than all those years ago. She was so understanding. She was absolutely amazing. She also tried to convince me to take the matter further and report him. She worried that he could still be hurting other young and vulnerable children, but unfortunately, at that moment in time, I knew I wasn't ready for that. I doubted anything would happen anyway, as there wasn't any evidence, so I had to put myself first and deal with this for myself and not for others, as selfish as this may sound. I can't thank my parents enough for how they have handled this; they have both been so supportive and strong for me, even though I know this is hurting them too.

My therapist also gave me some amazing advice during my sessions on how to let go of the character I had created. She suggested that I write Elle a letter, thanking her for getting me through all those hard times and how I couldn't have gotten through it without her help, but I am my own person now, and I knew I needed to face future situations as Josh and not as her anymore. It can be a dangerous mindset to develop as it can become toxic to have this character there in the mind for so long. I had Elle in my mind for ten years, mentally taking over sometimes when all I really wanted to be was myself. Working with my therapist, I have managed to let this character go and build enough strength that I can tackle situations myself without any need of mental assistance from a character that doesn't really exist. Of course there were times I didn't want to let Elle go; it was like having a best friend that had come into my life when something awful had just happened and then having to just let them go for no reason. But I knew that I needed to, for my own state of mind and to move on into my future.

As it stands now, writing this, I haven't yet taken any legal action with what happened to me. Personally, I don't feel I would get much out of it, the idea of making a statement and an investigation starting. The thought of the doctor being informed that I had made a statement against him. The process of the investigation. Having to tell my story again and again. Telling my story to someone whose role it may be to not believe me. Questioning whether people believe me and after all that the result could be something as simple as there wasn't enough evidence and it is simply my word against his. But he knows the truth, he knows what he did to me, and he has to live with that. One day, on his last day, he will look back on his life and know he isn't a good person and that self-doubt and self-punishment is enough justice for me right now. I want to focus on myself and moving on with life and leaving this horrible memory as that, a memory, the past. Yes, it has altered me and the way I see things, but no, it does not define me. With the help of my therapist, I have been practising safe-place training, which we have identified together as being completely still floating under the water, nobody around, complete silence and peace. With the practice of safe-place training and tapping meditation, I am slowly being able to calm myself down when feeling anxiety or stress. I really recommend this method for those who suffer from anxiety, panic attacks or stress. Each time you find yourself feeling this way, sit down, close your eyes and repeat light tapping anywhere on your body as you focus on the place you feel most safe. This place can be somewhere you have visited before or made up, but it is just a place, and you are alone there (if you place other people or animals here, it can cause future issues if you lose them). Ask yourself what can you see in this safe place? What do you hear here? What can you smell? Can you taste anything? Can you feel anything? As you focus on this safe place, continue tapping yourself over and over for a few moments. This method can be done privately or publicly as even on a train commute to work, somebody tapping on their fingers on their thighs doesn't draw attention.

CHAPTER FOUR

Education hadn't been the easiest road for me, my years in high school probably being the worst to experience, but that last year at high school was a highlight. I had been with the same group of girl friends throughout primary and high school, some joined us, and some left us, but some of us had stuck together since primary school. I also made some friends that I had outside of this group along the years at high school, some that I still talk to this day. Things at high school began to change for the better when I auditioned for the last school play of "Oliver Twist". Me and a couple of friends all auditioned (you'd think I would have been traumatised from the audition a few years previous), and we got our selected roles. I was originally cast as Noah, but during the script reading process, I didn't quite have the bullying characteristics mastered, so I was given the role of Mr Sowerberry, the creepy undertaker, instead. One of my friends from my group of girls had also auditioned, which made us become a lot closer than we already were, and this friendship seemed to cause rifts and friction within our friendship group. The two of us became inseparable and would run around calling ourselves "the twins". On my first day at high school, I remember spotting her in an RE lesson and thinking she was such a naturally pretty girl with the most ridiculous blue eyes. During the time rehearsing the play, the two of us became close to a new group of friends made up of other cast members. This group became so close that we were like a little family. A slightly bizarre family, as by the end of the school year, the majority of the group had begun having relationships with each other.

I'd had some girlfriends before, even in primary school, a puppy love relationship that went on for around 2 or 3 years. The majority of them didn't last very long at all, most of them no longer than a month. They were friendships, but we'd sometimes hold hands and maybe even hug, but it never resulted in anything more than a peck on the lips. Did I know I was gay as a teenager? Deep down somewhere, probably. But I managed to suppress this, and instead, in high school, I was very focused on wanting a girlfriend and being the perfect boyfriend. I had heard my group of female friends talk about what they wanted from their future boyfriends and the idea of the "perfect man". I wanted to be that. I wanted to step into that role and be exactly what people wanted me to be. This led me to my first long term relationship, which happened to be with my best friend with blue eyes (for the future of this book, we will call this person Sarah).

We were originally called "the couple that never happened" by our new group of friends. I was walking home from school one day with a friend that I had since primary school (this was actually the girlfriend I'd had throughout primary school). I can't remember how the conversation went, but somewhere in the conversation, something she said made me decide that I wanted to tell my best friend Sarah that I liked her more than a friend now. It was quite easy to do back then, all I had to do was update my MSN Messenger bio as "?????" followed by a love heart emoji and the question would be asked, "Who is that?" She was the first to ask that question. I remember being in my bedroom, getting excited as her username popped up on my laptop screen, and playing the game of "you need to guess who it is". She got there eventually and she wanted some time to think about it because she didn't believe that I really did like her. She'd had a crush on one of the boys, James, in our group of friends (James was actually the best man at my wedding), but I was hoping she'd decide to like me back.

I don't remember when we went from just being just friends to an official couple in a relationship, but eventually, she must have admitted that she liked me back and that was the start. I don't even remember our first kiss. I remember her Mum didn't seem quite so impressed when we became a couple and definitely made it clear as the years went on that she didn't view our relationship as a serious relationship, but more of a close friendship. In some ways, she was right, but at the time, I felt targeted and that I wasn't good enough for her daughter. Maybe I wasn't. I remember around the time of the 'Twilight' films being released, the character Edward was the "perfect boyfriend" image and I did everything I could to act just like Edward Cullen to her. I even set an alarm really early one morning, walked a 40-minute walk from my house to her Dad's house just so I could be there when she woke up like Edward was for Bella. Looking back now, it was a slightly embarrassing scenario as she had to tell her Dad what I was planning so he could let me in, but I thought it would be romantic and make me the perfect boyfriend to her. Her Dad was a typical "manly" man. He loved football and drinking, everything I wasn't. I did like him a lot, and we seemed to have a good bond whilst I was in a relationship with his daughter. He trusted me enough that he started to allow me to sleepover at his house. I was not allowed to stay over at her Mums, and if we were in her bedroom there, we had to keep the bedroom door open. There wasn't much reason not to trust us at that point, we may have had some heated moments of kissing and grinding our clothed bodies on each other, but we had never touched one another for until a few years into our relationship. She had expressed she wasn't ready for anything sexual and to be honest, neither was I. Some of our friends had had sex, but I didn't feel mature enough yet and of course, I knew the consequences of it. It also makes perfect sense that after the incident with the doctor, it had delayed my desire of exploring the world of sex for a little while. We were very young and very immature. There was a time when we had been watching a film and it had gotten heated whilst kissing. We had rolled around on top of the sheets and rubbed our clothed bodies against one another and that's as far as it went, but she spent the next 2–3 weeks googling, "can you get pregnant from dry humping?" The answer it gave her was "yes", which only made her panic more, but I knew that the chances were extremely slim and from what had happened between us, I knew we had no need to panic.

    Even though we were a couple by the spring, we spent most of our time with one of our really good friends, Olivia. A girl I still class as a really good friend today. We spent a lot of the spring and summer at each of our houses watching films and TV like 'America's Next Top Model', 'The Only Way Is Essex', 'Geordie Shore' and 'Gossip Girl', walking around the town, relaxing on the park in the sun with our group of friends. We were like the three amigos throughout that spring and summer.

I was really nervous getting ready to go to our leavers do (Prom) together. I stood there in my charcoal black suit that looked far too big on me, paired with a turquoise cravat that matched her dress perfectly and white floral patterned waistcoat. It felt like we were getting ready for a wedding rather than a leaver's do. She had been so excited for the day, booking in all her appointments for her hair, makeup and tan. She'd been trying to lose weight for her dress, with her Mum's encouragement and during the time leading up to this, I had been getting irritated because she wouldn't want to eat snacks with me as we watched films. She did look beautiful when she arrived at my house in her turquoise blue dress. I gave her a corsage made by my Mum's friend, and in my eyes, we looked like the perfect couple. I was playing the perfect boyfriend role, perfectly. But I can't say honestly I was always the perfect boyfriend. Looking back, I was very argumentative. I would get frustrated easily and storm out of her house, knowing I would be returning 5 or 10 minutes later. One of my biggest flaws is that I can be very argumentative and lose control of my temper. I can become angry over the smallest of things that aren't really worth wasting any energy on. I remember one time we had a petty argument at her Dad's house and as I stormed out, I purposely left my phone on the side, knowing that I would have to come back for it and then we could sort things out. Another time she had asked me to start jogging together in order to help her lose weight, but after not very long, I looked back and she had already given up and was walking. I took my frustration out on her instead of supporting her to continue on.

She was very aware of my struggles with mental health and she was one of the few people I would speak about it with. She knew that I had been or was still self-harming. She knew I had some days where I felt low and fed up and some days I felt completely distant from her because I would need my own space. She would take things personally a lot of the time and believe that I wasn't happy with her or that she wasn't good enough for me, but the reality was it wasn't her fault at all. There were demons I was dealing with that she could not control and she didn't know about.

Although I wasn't perfect, one thing I can give credit to myself for was I never pressured her into having sex. I have never agreed with anyone who did that.

Going into college together, there became a lot of pressure from other people for us to lose our virginity and have sex. We would get asked on a regular basis if we had yet and people seemed to roll their eyes and mock our relationship when we said we hadn't yet or that we were waiting. We decided just to tell people that we had to get people to stop asking us the same questions over and over and stop them questioning our relationship. We started to sexually experiment with one another sometime before we lost our virginities to each other. She was a very frigid girl and my private parts seem to absolutely terrify her. This wasn't helped when one day in college we sat in the canteen with our friends. The fake news had spread that we finally had sex and then a boy from our high school shouted over, "I'm surprised you can walk. I've seen his dick". And so, from that point on, my friends christened me with the nickname "10 Inch Finch", something I must say is a nickname I was proud of at the time. I had spent most of my school years hanging around with the girls, I didn't play sports, I wasn't the most masculine male out there, but as the nickname said, my penis was bigger than most of those masculine lads playing rugby and in a way, I felt like I'd won over them in some way. I had been accepted as one of the lads because of this. I absolutely loved being part of our group of friends; I felt like I belonged with them. I had a really great bond with the girls due to all my experience of hanging around with girls growing up, but I also had a good laugh with the boys and still have a really good friendship with James now. James and I made a promise to each other that we would be each other's best men when we got married (I'm happy to say we stuck to that promise). Sadly, as close we all were, I was never truly honest with my friends and never told them about my daily struggle with mental health issues.

Even when I decided not to return for the second year of college, the group still remained very close. We would have nights together, sleeping at each other's houses. It was during one of these nights that I had my first doubt of my sexuality. We all slept over at my Sarah's Mum's house, the living room was a circus of different duvets and pillows and we all ate snacks and drank very mild alcohol. We all eventually fell asleep. I was next to Sarah on my left, and to my right was one of the boys and his girlfriend. At some point during the night, I woke up and my friend had his foot slowly brushing up my leg. I wasn't sure at first if he was asleep or not, so I didn't move, but his foot moved to brush over my boxer shorts and I knew he was awake too. He kept brushing his foot over my boxers and could clearly feel I had developed an erection. I went to open my boxers to allow his foot to enter inside and he pulled his foot back quickly and pretended to be asleep. I was wide awake then. Curiosity was wild in my mind and I couldn't contemplate trying to sleep. I wanted more of this tense excitement. I adjusted myself, so I could reach and started to feel his leg too with my hand but pretended to be asleep as I did. I found my way to his boxers and could feel quite clearly he had an erection too. When my hand grasped around his erection, he jumped up and I pulled my hand back and the moment was over. My heart was racing and I panicked so much about what might happen. Had I just ruined my chances of staying in this group of friends? What if he denied touching me? What if I ended up losing my friends and my girlfriend. I had another panic attack that night as I escaped the room and went into the kitchen. My suspicions had been somewhat correct. I returned home the next day for a change of clothes. He spoke to Sarah and told her he thought I had felt him in the middle of the night. However, his girlfriend concluded it must have been her, and the issue was dropped. I did raise it with him one day during a college lesson we shared together. I told him how I had felt his foot on my boxers that night too, he simply laughed it off and said, "I didn't know I swung that way". That night was brought up a year or so later, in a conversation in a nightclub after drinking too much alcohol. I told him I had felt him feeling me and he admitted it and we laughed it off and never brought it up to one another again.

Nights in with friends turned into nights out. Once some of us had turned eighteen, we would go out together regularly in the local pubs and clubs, but of course, with alcohol, there comes trouble. One of the boys had cheated on one of the girls, and the group split into two. I stayed solidly in the middle, but I had my friends back and never even told Sarah when I knew what happened. As the college experience was coming to an end, the group slowly started to drift apart as one couple split up due to cheating, another split up for other reasons and it left me and Sarah the remaining couple. One girl had left the group of friends due to a falling out and others had drifted into other friendship groups. I can't remember when we all were last together, but I wish I could go back and tell our younger selves, "This is the last time you'll all be together" because I would have appreciated that moment a lot more. This group of people saved me in so many ways. They saved me from having another year of bullying and brutality and made me feel for the first time that I fit in somewhere. Even though some bullying had continued to some degree in college, one lad in particular targeted me with his shoulder barges for a short time and another girl would mock the way I spoke, shouting down the bus. I still belonged to my circle of friends and that meant a great deal.

I enjoyed drinking alcohol with my friends, but as I stated before, usually with alcohol comes trouble, the trouble for me was hiding my struggling sexual issues. During a night staying over at a friend's house, myself and my friend experimented with one another after drinking and watching pornography. After I had finished, I panicked instantly, saying I felt sick before rushing to the bathroom. I made myself physically sick and rang my brother asking him to pick me up as I didn't feel well. Before I left, my friend and I agreed to never bring this night up again and we haven't. I remember on the drive home feeling disgusting and extremely guilty that I had cheated on Sarah. I didn't feel good enough for her, so I suppressed any sexual confusion and I promised myself it wouldn't happen again.

I never quite felt accepted by Sarah's Mum. She always made it clear she believed I was getting in the way of her daughter's education. I was even banned from seeing her outside of school leading up to our GCSE and A-Level exams. Of course, a parent wants their child to have a great education, but it felt like she was being pushed so much that it wasn't what she wanted anymore but what she thought her Mum wanted for her. Her Mum would continuously put her down, especially about her weight, during our time together and this was something I started to really dislike causing an unspoken disagreement between us. There was once a time where Sarah was late for her period. She really panicked and wanted to go speak to a doctor. She even confided in my Mum before her own. I panicked too. It was very unlikely she was pregnant because we may have lost our virginity with one another, but I wouldn't really say that we had had sex. We were still learning, and so far, it just been a painful experience, physically and mentally. She refused to do a pregnancy test. She was scared of the answer and how it would affect her education, but eventually, her period came back on and the crisis was over. But the worst part was, she spoke to her own Mum about it and made her Mum aware that she had lost her virginity. I was given the whole "you don't touch my daughter again" speech from her, keeping my head down and agreeing to something ridiculous for the sake of not having an argument with a grown woman.

During this same year, we lost my Nan after only losing her husband, Grandad Tommy, the year before. Losing her was one of the hardest experiences of my life. I was incredibly close to my Nan. We all were. She was our rock in some way, shape or form. She was such an amazing woman, she could be telling you off and make you feel so incredibly loved in the same sentence and her laugh was infectious. I loved every minute I spent with my Nan and the conversations we had. I remember sitting by her bedside in hospital a week before she passed away and I asked her questions most people would be too scared to ask, but I asked her, "Are you scared to die?" She replied, "No, I'm tired of fighting now." I told her not to fight if she didn't want to, but she said she was fighting for her children. Her words were, "They want me to", but I told her she had to fight for herself and nobody else. She seemed so weak and in so much pain. She was on oxygen and it was causing sores around her lips and cheeks. I made her a promise that day and I've stuck to it ever since. I hope I've made you proud, Nan.

Nan made two requests before she passed away. To get her home so she can pass away in her own home and to bring her dog Megan to the hospital if we couldn't get her home to say their final goodbye. One day, my Mum got a phone call from the hospital advising her to come in to see her as they didn't think she had long left. Me and Mum ran to the car, and she drove erratically to get to the hospital as quickly as she could. She was crying and panicking that we wouldn't make it in time. She shouted at every red light, every slow driver and everyone indicating blocking up the road. I tried to calm her down and reminded her that everyone around us doesn't know what's happening to us. They were going about their normal day and had no idea that our world was crashing down. We all made it to the hospital, and a nurse agreed to turn away as my brother, and I brought Nan's dog Meghan in the hospital to see her. We smuggled her in, hidden under my hoodie, onto the ward to say a final goodbye to my Nan. But Nan surprised us all as she wasn't ready to say goodbye to us that night. Her condition did improve and the doctors were happy for her to have her final days at home. The night before she passed away, she had us all there, her children and their children and we all watched her favourite programme 'Mrs Brown Boys' and laughed together. The next morning after a drink of water, she said goodbye for the last time and took a piece of each of our hearts with her.

The lead up to her funeral was made much more difficult by my Sarah's Mum, who decided she didn't want her daughter to attend as it meant she would have to miss a day of college. She honestly believed a day of education was more important than supporting her boyfriend through one of the hardest days of his life so far. She compromised and allowed her to meet me at the service, but she had to go and get her morning attendance mark and then come for the service. At that point, I knew I did not like this woman, and she did not care for me.

Sarah enrolled in university and in all honesty, I think that was a signed deal. Our relationship was slowly coming to an end. She went to live in the city of Liverpool, it was only an hour away, but I didn't drive so couldn't go visit her. I remember how she struggled with homesickness that first few weeks; she asked me not to come up and visit her and allow her to get used to university life. In all honesty, I felt neglected back at home, but I knew it was what she needed. At this point, I had gone back to finish off my A-Levels, was juggling two part-time jobs, a barber and glass collector in a nightclub, trying to save money for my driving lessons and my first car. The weekend she moved into her halls of residence, I had been to college all day Friday, worked in the barbers late afternoon till evening, worked in the nightclub from evening till the early hours of the morning, slept for a few hours, returned to the barbers all day Saturday, returned to the bar Saturday evening until the early hours Sunday morning and then got up Sunday to help her move in to the halls of residence. Looking back now, I should have just given myself a lie-in instead. Her being away at university definitely changed our relationship a lot. I was getting away with hiding that I began to self-harm again as I was spending a lot of time on my own and started to really struggle with understanding myself. I had put so much pressure on trying to play the "perfect boyfriend" that I had set myself up for an inevitable fail. It's not something I've ever publicly admitted, but as she was away at university, I became unfaithful in our relationship. I had met up with strangers and let my teenage hormones get the better of me. In no way do I condone cheating. I really can't stress that enough and I have no excuse in any way, shape or form. She did not deserve to be cheated on. I can honestly say I don't think anyone gets away with cheating scratch-free, ever since I struggled with anxiety, trust issues, commitment issues and lack of self-worth. At one point, I couldn't even look at myself in a mirror where I worked and physically punched the mirror to smash it rather than look at myself any longer, hating what I saw. An injury to my fist I deserved. It was another way to self-harm, but this time, the addiction worsened and I became so much better at hiding it than I had been at school.

As all this was going on, James invited me into another circle of friends I had known from school but never really spoke to. We started to have regular nights out. I enjoyed being out with these friends at the weekend so much that when Sarah would come home from university to see me, I saw it as an inconvenience because I would have preferred to have been out with my friends drinking instead. I had decided from the time I started to be unfaithful that I was going to end my relationship with her, but being a coward, I kept delaying and delaying. At one point, I was halfway there on the motorway in my car, I planned to turn up at her halls and speak to her face to face, but I bottled it. The following weekend, she came home to visit me and I never mentioned that I had almost ended things.

I did become really moody around this time, and my argumentativeness with her definitely increased. One day I was in the barbers working when my Auntie, who worked for my Dad at the time, rang me to tell me that Dad had been rushed into hospital with a heart attack. I remember feeling like I was going to physically throw up. I rang Sarah to update her, and she begged me to come to pick her up first and we'd go visit my Dad together. We got in the car, my old 2001 plate Renault Clio and got on the motorway—I had hardly been on the motorway before this point, and the ones I had experienced were one junction on and then one junction off. She had the address up on her phone, following the map's directions, but she was getting really confused and frustrated as time went on, so my frustration with her only grew. After finally getting off the motorway—I was driving on the wrong side of the road at one point—we had to do several U-turns and got stopped by a few closed roads, so I pulled into a hotel car park to check the map myself. As I turned the ignition off, the key snapped in the ignition. Of course, this technically wasn't her fault, but in my frustration, I blamed her for making us get to this point, a point I may lose my Dad and not be there to say goodbye. We sat outside the hotel for hours, waiting for recovery to pick us up, who then told us we needed a locksmith, so we had to wait even longer. It was very warm that day, the hotel receptionist came out with some juice and biscuits for us whilst we waited. I was raging with anger and channelling it on her for making us pull over in the first place. She admitted later that she thought there was no going back for us at that point. Luckily, we got to the hospital hours, and hours later, my Dad made a full recovery and I finally got rid of the 2001 Renault Clio a few short months later, ironically around the same time, our relationship came to an official end.

    I decided that it would be our last Christmas together. I knew how much she loved Christmas, so I didn't want to ruin it for her. Instead, I wanted to make it the best Christmas she could have. I spent a fortune on presents for her that year. One of my new friends said, "Why you spending all this money when you are going to finish her?" But I felt like she deserved one last good Christmas together and I felt like I needed to be the "perfect boyfriend" one last time. Just after Christmas, she had gone back to university when I made the phone call whilst out driving on my own. I cried, and she cried, but she understood. Our four year relationship had run its course and the only thing left to do was split up so we could keep our friendship. Sadly, that wouldn't survive for very long either.

CHAPTER FIVE

2015 was a very complicated year for me. It's a year that changed everything. Everything I have written about in this book up until now, though I see almost like a past life like I wasn't really there or connected to myself around this time. I can see pictures of my younger self, I know that they are me, but I have separated myself from myself then and myself now. 2015 was a bridge in-between the two lives. In conversations I have had with people over time, many have discussed having the one year that they went "wild" or "crazy", but they are referring to they partied, drank a lot, took many drugs, or had a lot of promiscuous sex. I did some of those things too during this year, but this year for me was wild and crazy for all other reasons. It was a year that was the best and the worst year of my life. Many things happened to me over this year, so the events are split over the next four chapters, each chapter focusing on the key elements that made up that year.

At the start of the year, I ended my relationship with Sarah, and we had decided we would remain good friends. We once had a conversation as we drove around in my car, that although we had lost our sexual love for one another, we still wanted our best friend back again, the person we had had by our side back in high school together and I really did want that. There was nothing I wanted more at the time; I would have loved to have had her back as a really good friend. But most people learn, keeping an ex as a friend is never really for the long term, and it comes with many complications. One complication was that we continued to be sexual with each other, something a lot of people do when their relationship is over, but of course, it adds confusion to the equation. One evening I was at the cinema with my friends and she was at a family party—this was the first family event I hadn't gone to when I normally would. The film we were watching had such a dramatic and emotional ending that I felt like it was a sign that I wanted to give our relationship another go and I got swept up in these emotions. I texted her to tell her I wanted to talk about things and she asked me to come to join them at the party. Once the film finished, I made my way to the party venue, greeted by her and her little sister. Her Mum was clearly not thrilled to see me back on the scene. I can hold my hands up and admit this definitely would have been confusing for Sarah. Did it mean we were getting back together? I had no idea, to be honest; I was just as confused too. That night we were intimate together once again—at this point, we were still struggling to have intercourse, so we usually found other ways to be intimate.

The year previous to our break-up, I returned to college to finish my A-Levels studies. During my second year of college, I became really good friends with two girls. One was a beautiful mixed-race girl (she will be named Gabrielle for this book). Sarah was incredibly jealous and cautious of my friendship with her. The other was blonde-haired (we will name her Jodie) and two years younger than me. Sarah had no concern at all for her, but that was who did threaten our relationship. Jodie and I became such good friends. We would harmlessly flirt together during our lessons and would say phrases like "you're my back up" or "I'm waiting for you to leave her". It was like it had become an agreement that once I split up with Sarah, the two of us would start something more than friendship. After college, I enrolled at the same university as Sarah had been going to. I believed that if I went the same one as her, it may help us rebuild that connection again, but of course, I knew that I hadn't been faithful to her, and this destroyed our relationship for me, so I ended things just three months after enrolling at the university. The night before the cinema trip with my friends, I had been out drinking with them, when I bumped into Jodie, we did have a kiss that night, but nothing more happened. I let Gabrielle and Jodie know that I had decided to see how things would go with Sarah during a night out together.

Jodie wasn't remotely impressed and had to be calmed down by Gabrielle whilst she screamed at me. I felt bad. Was I stringing two girls along? I hadn't meant to, but I also knew I wasn't being appropriate and definitely wasn't being "the perfect boyfriend" to either of them.

But giving things another go with Sarah didn't last very long either. This time the friendship was destroyed along with it. We went for some food near the university campus and we started to have a disagreement over my group of friends. She felt like they were changing me and that my best friend (we will call him Charlie) was the leader of the group controlling how we all acted (she was right—but we will get to that later). I obviously stuck up for Charlie, my friends and myself and defended our friendship which she didn't like to hear. She started to accuse me of treating her "like shit" for the past four years, which hurt because although I knew I hadn't been perfect, I was trying to be, but deep down, I knew she was right because I had been unfaithful to her, so I got more defensive with it. As it came to paying the bill, I sulkily told her, "since we aren't together, we can split it". After years of the bill being paid for her, she told me she hadn't even brought her purse. The fact that she had assumed I was just going to pay for her after the argument we had just had was enough for me. I walked out, her walking behind me the whole way, got into my car and drove home away from the campus and that was the end of our relationship and our friendship. We removed one another and each other's family members and friends from social media, but we were still in each other's lives for months afterwards, but for all the wrong reasons. The drama. I had people telling me during nights out with my friends that things were being said about me by her and her friends and weren't true. One rumour was that I had been showing naked photos of her (I didn't have any naked photos of her to show). Another girl told me she had been told I had forced her into having an abortion (she had never been pregnant during our relationship, and no abortion ever took place, to my knowledge). A customer from work told me she had been telling him that I treated her vile for years and another mutual friend claimed that she would tell people I had been following her. I'd had enough of the lies and went straight from work to her Dad's house to ask her to stop spreading lies, but she wasn't there. Her Dad said he'd pass the message on to her.

One day I got back home and my phone had lost charge and was taking a while to restart. Sarah had bought me an iPad the previous Christmas, but I hadn't used it much and eventually put it away in a drawer. I decided to check to see if the iPad had any remaining charge on it whilst I waited for my phone to turn back on, and surprisingly, it did. I was scrolling down social media, seeing the same names coming up with updates on their life when a message popped up from a mutual friend of mine and Sarah's. The message read, "He's acting so fake, I don't recognise him anymore". This message was about me and wasn't meant for me to see. I noticed then the small avatar where my profile picture should have been instead was Sarah's profile picture. I was on her account. She must have been on the iPad last and left her account logged in. Should I have logged out straight away and respected her privacy? Absolutely! Did I? Absolutely not! I could have snooped a lot more than I did, but I genuinely, hand on heart, did not. I did look to see if she had been talking to any boys recently, which she had not and then continued to allow messages to come through from her friends, leaving the ones I wasn't interested in unopened, but if my name was mentioned, I would have a look. After a few weeks of this happening, she lied to some of her university friends and said that me and my friends had been following her on nights out and sitting by the park near her house—we did sit in the park when the weather was nice, but we had done that before me and she split up and we never followed her on any of the nights out. In all honesty, I didn't want to follow her because it would stop my chances of being able to enjoy myself with other girls. At this point, I was more than done with the lies and confronted her directly. I texted her and asked her to stop lying about me to people. When she denied any knowledge, I sent over screenshots of the conversation I had just watched unfold, knowing full well I was showing her I was logged into her account. It wasn't long before her parent's turned up at my house, demanding to speak to me. I was very hesitant to allow her Mum to come through the front door, but her Dad had been decent with me, so I stepped aside for him to come in. My Mum came downstairs and invited her Mum inside and we sat in the living room discussing the matter. I showed them that I had logged out of her social media and explained what had happened and why I had stayed logged in. Her Dad was quite understanding and said he just wanted all the arguing between us to be over, as I did too. Her Mum was there to cause more trouble and threatened me with "don't come near our house or that park again or else".

Luckily, the others heard the threat and attitude towards me too and asked them to leave not before another threat was made telling me, "Don't dare go out next weekend and ruin her birthday with her friends!" That's how ridiculous things got between us.

During this writing process, I have learnt a lot about myself and looking back. I do regret some of my actions towards the break up with Sarah. The weekend of her birthday, I should have listened and stayed away, not because I was threatened to—because it was the decent thing to do—but played the cocky teenager role well even though my friends had already arranged to have a night out that weekend. A few of her friends came up to me in a nightclub, either giving me abuse or asking me to leave, but I couldn't see what I was doing wrong as I was out drinking with my friends and honestly wasn't remotely interested in what she was doing. But of course, she got upset and I would instantly become the "bad guy". Another weekend, I was out drinking with friends again when I saw her with her cousin. That night I got myself stupidly drunk. I could hardly string sentences together. I was in an absolute state. She walked past me and I stupidly shouted over, "No more lies please, darling". That should have been enough to realise the fact that I wasn't being myself as I had never used the phrase "darling" in my life. One of my friends pulled me away as we started to argue. As they did, I embarrassingly shouted, "I cheated on you anyway", a sentence I am very grateful ever since that she never heard as it would have caused her a lot of pain and embarrassment at the time. Another statement that I regret saying that night was, "Go get the same medication as your Mum". I shouted during our argument. I can't stress enough that I still regret it to this day as nobody should have their mental health used against them in an argument. This very same night, as we moved onto another nightclub, a friend of hers was working. She came up and asked me to leave because I was upsetting her friend. I refused to leave, drunkenly not understanding why I had to leave, so she got a bouncer to deal with me instead. He insisted I leave immediately, and as I did, I cockily threw them some insults. Ironically, the girl who worked at the nightclub is now my sister-in-law and we have come a very long way from being thrown out of a nightclub because of an ex-girlfriend being upset.

After the split with Sarah, I wanted some time to enjoy myself, so I signed up for a dating app and met up with a few different girls, but nothing came of it. I was almost certain at that point that I would end up in a relationship with Jodie, my friend from college, but although she had questioned sometimes what was happening between us, I didn't want to rush straight into another relationship. What I wasn't expecting to happen was my friendship with Charlie from my group of friends to overstep the boundary of friendship. The two of us had become extremely close after I split up with Sarah. He had encouraged me to do so, I had a lot more time dedicated to my friends, so we inevitably ended up becoming very close. He would try to tease me and tell me who had been his favourite friend that night. I'd always want to be his favourite and I loved feeling like I was his favourite in the group. He started to pick me up first just so I could sit in the front with him and then he would drop me off last so we could talk in the car till the early hours of the morning. At one point, one of our friends said we acted like a couple with how close we were and I believe that was the point our friendship started to change. I was jogging one day when he rang to tell me what our friend had said about our friendship. We made a joke of it and said we would have to pretend to not be as close, so people didn't get suspicious of us, but we'd carry on being incredibly close in secret. It had started as a joke between us, calling it our "secret affair", but I didn't think it would ever end up the way it did. At this point, my life felt great. I was still dealing with some of my demons, but I enjoyed my life for the first time. I felt accepted by this group of lads. I had become one of the lads and wasn't being judged for not liking sports; they actually seemed to enjoy that I didn't and would try to educate me on the teams, the players and betting. I always hid my self-harming addiction, especially from them and my family, but I was coping a lot better than I had been years previously.

My parents were away one weekend to celebrate my Mum's birthday. My eldest brother Adam was staying at his girlfriend Rachael's and my brother Connah was living in Ibiza so I had a free house for the weekend, so I decided to use this weekend to celebrate my birthday with my friends. We planned to go to Liverpool for a night out together and then they could all stay over at my house afterwards. Nothing was out of the ordinary during the night, we drank a lot of alcohol, and we took pictures and funny videos together. We didn't touch drugs. When we got back home in the early hours of the morning, we went to bed; Charlie was lying next to me on the floor. I woke up the next morning and his arm was around me, his body was curved around mine, spooning me and I could feel his erection against my back. Of course, this isn't unusual, it is something that males can't always control first thing in the morning, but when I adjusted my arm so that my hand was resting against it and he didn't move even though he was awake, my suspicions started that he was feeling the same as I was. Maybe we could have this "secret affair".

We didn't talk about it much from that day, but more events occurred over the weeks that made us go beyond just being friends. I was staying over at my cousin's house one weekend as her parents were away with her little brother. She had asked me to stay as she felt safer than being home alone. She wanted to go to the pub to see her friends in the evening. I told her I would go out with my own friends too and then we could meet back at her house for a certain time. We both got back late and she gave permission for Charlie to stay over too, she went to bed and we stuck on a scary movie. I'm not sure when but I ended up laying at the side of him with my hand on his chest whilst he ran his hands through my hair—not the usual position that two male best friends would watch a film together in. We set up a double duvet on the living room floor as we got ready to go to sleep, he began to tickle my back with his fingers, and it felt really nice. He added more and more pressure until it was feeling more like an intense sports massage and I started to physically moan painfully, he seemed to enjoy that and he started whispering into my ear, "Do you like that?" Nothing more sexual happened other than we were both erect. The next day my back was completely covered in bruises from his "tickling", again this sight seemed to please him, but on the way back home, we decided not to tell our friends about what had happened over the weekend as we knew they would "misunderstand".

But things took a dramatic turn one night, and all the tension we had been building up between us finally took over. We were on a night out drinking with our friends in the nightclub we usually went to when he whispered into my ear, "Are we going yours and having this secret affair then?" Of course, I agreed and we left without even saying bye to our friends. I don't remember how it started and I don't remember who made the first move, but I do remember being naked in bed together and kissing, thinking, "What the fuck is happening!" This was Charlie's first time with anyone. We woke up the next morning very hungover and agreed that we would never do or speak about it again. But we did. We did pretty much every time we went out on a night out together. We agreed it would only happen whilst we had been drinking, but it started to happen whilst we were sober too. We would drop all our friends off at their homes after spending the evening in the car and then we would pull up somewhere to enjoy one another. We even went inside my house once in the early hours of the morning and had sex in the living room whilst my parents were upstairs in bed. There was a time in my bedroom when it was incredibly late and I actually fell asleep during it and was speaking gibberish in my sleep, but we carried on anyway. We did it in the place I worked at too. We had spent the night before together and got up late, so I didn't have time to take him home in the morning, so he came to work with me. Instead of working that day, I locked the door and we went into the back room and caught up on our sleep and the rest (if the owner of that shop is reading this, I can only apologise for the lack of profit that day).

One weekend, I stayed with him at his Mum's boyfriend's house, she took her boyfriend away, I think it was Barcelona. When they got back from their holiday, I was having a conversation with his Mum and I could see in her eyes that she knew what was going on between us. Our friends may not have clicked on, but our parents were starting to become suspicious. My Mum had become very accustomed to Charlie staying over and would shout upstairs asking if he wanted breakfast, sometimes surprised when he wasn't there. We became very risky about where we crossed the line of friendship. One night we all went to one lad's house for pre-drinks during a night with friends, but Charlie got far too drunk and started being sick. Everyone decided it was best to put him to bed on the couch. I was sitting next to him, his legs resting on top of mine and once we were alone, he asked me to stay with him when they all headed out to town. I accepted the invitation. Once they all left, we stayed on the couch and we calmly pleasured one another. Just in case they came back earlier than planned, we didn't let it get too intense. After they all returned in the early hours, the lad who hosted offered the bedrooms upstairs for us all to sleep in. Me and Charlie selected the sister's room and got into bed with each other, trying not to arouse any suspicion. We did have sex that night, keeping the noise to a minimum, but we were disturbed in the morning by a hungover friend who had decided to join us in the bed to have a chat with us. He was oblivious to the fact that the whole time he was talking to us, we continued what we had been doing under the covers right next to him. It was almost impossible to keep a straight face and hold the noises of pleasure in.

We decided to nickname our situation "the box" and if we ever felt like we needed to discuss anything about it over text, it had to be coded as "the box". The codeword "the box" came from me, saying it was something we needed to put in a box in our minds and ignore whenever our friends were around. I'd be lying if I didn't say I completely fell for him. I loved how it felt being around him, I wanted to be his favourite, and this secret affair proved I was his favourite—until I wasn't.

My brother Connah lived in Ibiza for the majority of that year and I decided on a whim that I would go over and see him there. I asked Charlie to come with me, but he couldn't arrange it with work in time, so I went over solo. I remember my Mum was extremely worried about me flying for the first time in years on my own. Since our last family holiday to Turkey, I hadn't left the United Kingdom the year my Gran had passed away. But I felt pretty confident in going; I wanted to see Ibiza. After all, I was a single young lad and it was what young single lads did, wasn't it? I spent the night before I went with Charlie in the car and he dropped me back off at home just a couple of hours before I was due to leave for the airport. I didn't sleep until I was on the plane. Ibiza wasn't the right place for me. I was happy to see my brother, and he seemed happy to have me there. He walked me around, showing me places and introduced me to people he knew, but overall I was really disappointed in what I saw there. The weather was not as good as I thought and didn't help with the experience. We spent the afternoon around a pool and I watched with my headphones in as people were dancing and drinking, but I noticed people were also buying drugs. I'd seen people doing drugs back home, but the whole environment always made me feel really uncomfortable. That was the first sign I didn't want to stay there. The second was due to Charlie; he texted me telling me his Mum had spoken to my Mum in the supermarket and they had been talking about our bond and relationship and he was suspicious of what I had told my Mum. I reassured him I had never told my Mum anything about our secret affair, but he was angry with me, which triggered my already increasing anxiety. I wasn't his favourite now. He was angry with me. He said I was disappointing him. His next set of texts completely threw me off. He told me they had arranged to go to the Trafford Centre and that he was really looking forward to spending time with them without me being there. I went along with the conversation, trying not to be oversensitive and said it would be good for him, and he made it clear that I was losing my rank of being his favourite by being away from him. I went upstairs to my brother's shared apartment, locked myself away in the bathroom and had a severe panic attack. I could feel myself trembling and trying to get rid of the feeling. I eventually made myself vomit. It didn't work. I told my brother I was feeling tired from travelling and told him to go on to a party that night without me. As he started getting ready, I looked online at flights home. I booked the first flight I could find, but now I had to tell my brother I was going home already. He seemed really hurt and concerned. I felt awful that he thought it was something to do with him. I'm sorry, Connah, this had nothing to do with you at all. This was a collection of too many things going on in such a short space of time. He rang my Mum, who I had been avoiding contact with all day, and she instantly FaceTimed me. I got upset straight away and confessed the panic attack to her; she insisted I came home. I did exactly 24 hours in Ibiza, leaving first thing in the morning, making it home in time to go to the Trafford Centre with Charlie and our friends. I sat in the back of the car, the lads all laughing at my bizarre 24 hours, I looked over at Charlie driving and he had this smug smile on his face and I knew at that point, he'd won, I had done exactly what he wanted from me, he knew he had control over me. If he said "jump", I would have said, "how high". I was completely in his control. But I didn't achieve what I had wanted to. I was no longer the favourite. At the time, I put it down to the conversation with our Mums must have freaked him out and scared him off a little, but now I believe he'd done what he wanted with me and no longer needed me at the top spot.

Our secret affair only lasted around 4 to 5 months, but of course, it would come to an end at some point. My only hope was that we would remain best friends afterwards and I wouldn't lose the group of friends that had accepted me. I couldn't lose any more people. But of course, this "crazy" year wouldn't have been as traumatic as it was if we lived happily ever after.

I had still been picking my potential love interest, Jodie, up from work once a week and we'd talk about potentially getting together one day, but nothing seemed to be going forward with it. I was too wrapped up in Charlie to make any sort of effort with her anymore. On Sunday, she texted me to say she didn't need a lift home the next day and that she had sorted one. Being the arrogant and cocky teen, I was, I didn't really care that much that she had cancelled on me—I wasn't really that invested in the potential relationship anymore. The relationship I was invested in seemed like it was going to progress to a new strength when Charlie texted me, asking if we could talk. I was convinced this would be the moment he was going to say that he wanted to be together, not to tell everyone but be committed to each other. I was so excited and I couldn't wait to hear the words come out of his mouth. But those weren't the words I heard, the words I did hear made me feel sick to my stomach and I physically felt the colour drain from me. He confessed he had been talking to someone and that someone was Jodie. The two of them had been texting each other for a couple of weeks and didn't tell me. The most complicated love story there was—imagine if Edward Cullen and Jacob Black were secretly sleeping together whilst also spending their time with Bella Swan.

I'd love to say he was very apologetic about the situation, but instead, he tried to make me feel bad about myself by telling me I had no right to be angry with either of them and I hadn't been fair stringing her along and never done anything about it. He was right in some way, but in my eyes, a friend doesn't start texting and seeing the girl their mate has been having a potential relationship with, especially when you've been sleeping with that friend for a few months. I had nobody to vent to, nobody that could know the full extent to why I was so angry with him and once again, I felt completely alone and my mental health started to become chaotic. At the time, jogging and running definitely helping suppress my anxiety, but there were only so many runs I could fit into one day, so I turned back to self-harming and it became excessive, even doing it whilst at work using my work tools to hurt myself, just to release some of the building anxiety from me. The pain meant to be a distraction from my thoughts and a distraction from the hurting inside. I convinced myself that I deserved this and deserved to be betrayed by someone because I had betrayed Sarah, this was my karma, and I deserved every ounce of pain that I was feeling.

I confided some of my worries (leaving out the secret affair) to one of my friends from the group about how Charlie had started to talk to Jodie. Thankfully he agreed it wasn't what friends did to each other. I was relieved that at least one of those lads was going to be on my side. Or so I thought he was. Instead, this friend became Charlie's new favourite and the two of them made it clear within the next couple of months that they didn't have much time for me anymore. I spoke to my therapist about my anxieties around Charlie, she suggested maybe writing some questions down and voicing them to him, but that didn't go to plan. The questions included questions about how he felt about us, how he felt about the situation with Jodie, how he thought I would feel and what he planned for the future for the three of us. We had been out with our friends in the car. I dropped him off last so I could explain about the suggested advice and if I could ask him this list of questions. He agreed to hear the questions, but he refused to answer every single one. I desperately begged him to be open and honest with me, explaining that it will either make me feel better or give me the closure I need to move on, but he repeatedly refused to answer. He didn't want me to feel better and that became clear.

Not much time after Charlie and Jodie made their relationship official, they started to sleep together too. I made it my mission to see if I could still win him over and be his favourite, get back to how we were before the night he told me he was talking to her. I did win. I won twice after the two of them made their relationship official, me and him spent the night together, once in the car and once in my Dad's office (sorry, Dad!). We were there printing posters for his Mum's boyfriend's birthday. Somehow we ended up lying under the desk chatting and it soon turned to be playing with one another. He refused to kiss me this time because of his new relationship, but he was quite happy for everything else.

All our friends praised how well I handled the situation and being ok with Charlie dating the girl I was sort of seeing. They didn't know that I was emotionally drained inside and didn't know where I could turn to. One night, we had a conversation in the car, just him and me. He asked about my depression, how it felt low like I had done, and how it affected me. His conclusion was, "I couldn't be arsed living like that". I agreed and said it was difficult sometimes. He responded back with, "I'd kill myself me"—I'm not passing blame to anyone here. I'm not saying any future events were anyone else's responsibility. I am a grown adult, and I made every decision myself, but I felt he wanted me to act on this during this conversation. After speaking to my therapist years later, I now understand that I was a problem he wanted rid of. Why? Because I was the only other person in the world who knew our secret. So I took steps back. I turned to Sarah like a comfort blanket. I texted her to see if we could meet up to talk one night—this annoyed Charlie when he found out. I didn't tell her that anything had happened with him, just that he had started to date, Jodie. She was really shocked at this and expressed how she had never trusted him as a friend to me–little did she know the real story was even more hurtful. I confessed to her that night what had been happening with Jodie around the time me and her had been separating. She did say this hurt her a little and made her feel like a "mug", but we decided to try giving being friends a go again, now some time had passed. We talked for hours, talked about a boy she had been dating, I told her about a few girls I'd texted and spoken to. She confided in me about how she had become extremely obsessed with losing weight. This obsession had started in the last year of a relationship. It felt really nice to have someone come back into my life rather than a void where they had once been. She was filling the void that Charlie and Jodie were slowly beginning to leave.

CHAPTER SIX

Towards the end of the year, I admitted to myself and others that I was struggling mentally and went to the doctors to ask for some help. I was immediately prescribed the antidepressant Sertraline. The medication didn't agree with me, my anxiety only getting worse to the point I struggled stomaching food and usually would vomit within an hour of eating, sometimes making myself be sick (please note I wasn't making myself be sick because I disliked myself or the way I looked it was because I hated the feeling of waiting to be sick). I didn't know then the effects of bulimia and the dangerous risk it posed. Within a month of being prescribed Sertraline at the age of 20, I was weighing six stone and two pounds. My outside form started to resemble how I was feeling on the inside, weak. Around this time, my friends and I began to experiment with smoking weed. They had me arrange to buy it from a customer at work, and we'd smoke it in the car and at each other's houses. It seemed like a good idea at the time, I was hoping it would calm my nerves and my anxious thoughts, but it had the opposite effect, it did nothing positive for my anxiety or mental health and I started to come across as erratic.

Both me and Sarah were invited to our friend Olivia's 21st birthday party. We had been three amigos back in high school and I was looking forward to us spending some time together again. I was a little apprehensive about attending as I knew Sarah's Mum was going to be there too, and I didn't have the support of my friends there. I decided not to drink that night with the tense atmosphere and awkward post-relationship/friendship and my deteriorating mental health. Adding drink into the equation wouldn't be smart. Something I wish everyone in the situation had also considered. Sarah's Mum was her usual self, very critical of me; she went out of her way to try making me feel uncomfortable and turned argumentative once she saw I wasn't reacting, asking me, "What are you even doing here? Nobody wants you here" I wasn't going to let our drama ruin Olivia's birthday party, so I left straight away. Getting home, I started to explain what had happened to my parents when I got a text from Olivia explaining Sarah's Mum had been asked to leave because she was causing trouble and being ridiculously drunk, so she wanted me to come back and continue the birthday celebrations with her. I wish I would have stayed at home, but I didn't. I got back in my car and returned to the party. Some of our high school friends were entering the party as I got there. One of the girls went out of her way to wait for me so we could enter together. It should have been that simple—just friends walking in together—but unfortunately, it wasn't simple, instead as I walked into the venue, Sarah's Mum hadn't left just yet. She had been waiting outside with her boyfriend and Sarah's Dad. They saw me entering and shouted over warnings to me, I chose to ignore them and continue on, but they didn't want that. They wanted an argument with me, and before I knew it, I had both of Sarah's parents screaming and shouting in my face. Her Dad shocked me. Since the break-up, he'd been decent with me but now was threatening me with physical violence if I caused his daughter any more pain. Her Mum's comments were absolutely vile. She told me that she wished I had died and continuously called me a "freak" for being addicted to self-harming. The comment that topped it off was "go home and slit your wrist. You freak", all in front of a lot of people I had kept my mental health issues from.

 My mind couldn't handle it anymore and I just emotionally shut down. I just turned my emotions off and went through the motions of the night without processing what had just happened. Someone pulled me away from them, still shouting and screaming after me and Sarah Mum's boyfriend pulled her away as her Dad continued pointing his finger in my face, with his face all screwed up in anger. There was complete and utter silence as I stepped into the party room.

There were a few awkward minutes of silence before the music was turned back on. I knew that everyone knew what had just gone on outside. Sarah had been told what had happened and was emotionally apologetic to how they had been with me. I thought she could have come out and explained to them that she did want to be friends too, and it wasn't just me, but I think it was easier for her to let me take the blame.

But the drama didn't stop there. Sarah asked me if I would take her home after the party, so I accepted, but her friend didn't think it was a good idea. I reassured her friend that I hadn't drunk anything and that she would be perfectly fine with me. Her friend expressed to Sarah that she didn't trust me and didn't trust her being around me. Everybody was painting me as some villain, I knew I had made some mistakes, I knew the break up had become messy, but in no way was I completely to blame for it all—we both had acted immature with our break up and we both could have made life easier for one another, but we chose to try win points against each other instead. Her friend rang her own parents and they came to collect her, but they had come to collect Sarah too on her Mum's orders. Sarah's friend's Mum sat down next to me, talking quietly to me so that nobody could hear, she said "Do you know I've never liked you? So you can just fuck off!" I responded back with, "You can fuck off too". Her husband squared up to me when he heard me. We were face to face me when I defended myself and explained that I had every right to return the phrase to his wife if she had originally told me to fuck off. They were asked to leave too and took their daughter and Sarah with them. When I left, I was escorted to my car by a friend in case all the threats made towards me that night became more than just threats. As soon as I got into the car, I turned the radio off, my head was banging in pain, and all I needed was silence, but the silence only allowed for my thoughts to run wild in my head, and I didn't have the strength to stop the abusive comments from Sarah's Mum, "go home and slit your wrist you freak" and "wish you'd died" replaying over and over again, getting louder each time. I'm surprised I made it home because I have no recollection of that journey other than the replaying of comments, they blinded me, and I had gone into auto-pilot mode, getting myself home without paying any attention to the roads. My Mum and Dad were already in bed when I got home, the house was silent too and there was still no distraction from my thoughts. I got into bed, but the thoughts just wouldn't stop, "go home and slit your wrist you freak", "wish you'd died", "go home and slit your wrist you freak", "wish you'd died", "go home and slit your wrist you freak", "wish you'd died". I couldn't stop them and I couldn't get to sleep. My head wouldn't turn off the thoughts, and I stopped thinking rationally and started to panic, wondering would they ever stop? Was I losing my mind? I needed them to stop; I couldn't handle listening to them anymore. I didn't want to listen to them anymore. How could I make them stop? Then I decided. My Mum had some sleeping tablets in the medicine cupboard. If I took one of them, hopefully, it could knock me out. I went downstairs and took one tablet and then I took another, and another, and another. I don't know how many I took, but I took the box and also took the box of paracetamol upstairs with me and I lay there and waited for the silence to come.

    I honestly don't remember much from that point, other than the feeling of pain in my lungs and feeling warm, too warm; it was a rush of intense heat. My brother, Connah, heard me being sick from his bedroom and found me on the bathroom floor. My memory is very distorted from that night, but I remember being on the bottom step of the stairs with someone holding me up, my Mum shouting to my Dad in the living room, telling him to tell the ambulance to hurry up. They were advised to keep me awake so both my brothers held me up and tried making me walk. My Mum has told me since that each time I woke up, I would cry, "I'm not a freak, Mum", or "she called me a freak". In the ambulance, I could hear my Mum crying whilst praising me to the paramedic. I was hurting her. I understood at this point what I'd done; I didn't want to hurt anyone I had just wanted everything to stop, my thoughts, my feelings, my pain to stop. I don't think I necessarily want to die in that moment of taking the tablets; I was just trying to make everything stop for a moment. Pause. But there was no way to pause life, so I decided to press the stop button instead. I remember nothing after that. My Mum explained that my oxygen levels were low and my kidney and liver weren't working probably, so I had to be placed on oxygen, and my heart rate was low, so it had to be monitored. My Mum would shake me each time my heart rate was dropping. She was scared I was slipping away in my sleep. I vaguely remember hearing her talk about my Sarah's Mum and the things she had said to me. The next thing I remember, I was back at home in my own bed, the bed I should have died in the night before. When I woke up, I wasn't sure if anything that had happened was real. I let the memories flood back as I lay there. My lungs were still aching but not as intensely, and my joints felt weak. I went to grab my phone from the bedside table but my phone not being there was clarification that it was real. I was still here, I was alive and I wasn't sure how I felt about that. I went downstairs to all my family in the living room. They stared at me as I walked into the room. My feet were dragging on the floor as I felt really weak. I stood there looking back at their staring eyes and asked, "What?". It was a stupid question. My Mum started to cry and say "I'm so sorry". My first thought was, am I dead? Had I died last night, and for some strange reason, they can all see my ghost? The next sentence completely shocked me, as my Mum told me that she had beaten up Sarah's Mum for what she had done to us. I say us, because my suicide attempt didn't just affect me that night, it affected my whole family and it's something that we still are recovering from now. My Mum explained that after they had brought me home from the hospital and put me in bed, they drove around to Sarah's Mum's house to confront her over her actions at Olivia's party. It had been the really early hours of the morning, and they had to be woken up by the knocking at the front door. I believe there was some refusal of a conversation but eventually, the door was opened and it eventually led to my Mum punching her repeatedly in the face as she screamed, "I've done nothing wrong". She had no idea of the pain that she had caused, that her words had almost taken a life away, my Mum's little boy's life away. I do not condone violence in any way, shape or form and this is something my Mum has regretted from the moment it had happened, I know that for a fact. I am not a parent and I have no idea how I would react if someone's words had almost taken my child away from me, so I won't ever judge my Mum on her actions that day. One thing that can be said about my Mum is that she allows herself to be pushed around, bullied and walked all over, but she will not allow this to happen to her children. My Mum did stop as Sarah came running down the stairs shouting for her to stop and as she sat down on the sofa my Mum knelt down in front of her and told her what had happened to me and why it had happened. She asked Sarah to explain to her own family and others that her illness of bulimia was not my fault and Sarah agreed herself it was not. One thing my Mum noticed from their conversation was she never asked if I was ok. Something that has hurt me ever since. I checked to see if she had been online on her social media the moment my phone was given back to me, she had, but I hadn't received a message or anything from her to see if I was ok. Did she not care? I did have a text from Charlie. The text was simple "Let me know when you are awake". I texted him back to say I was at home and awake and he arranged for me to see my friends that afternoon. I was only allowed to leave the house if I was being collected, so once my parents saw Charlie's car, they allowed me to go be with my friends. They all seemed very concerned, shocked and confused. I explained to them that I had been struggling with depression and anxiety for a very long time and the conflict from the night before had tipped me over the edge. It felt more normal being back with my friends, back to normal life instead of the chaos of being close to death. Still, I could tell this had spooked them all and they were completely entitled to feel that way, but for the first time in a very long time, I felt isolated and lonely again, even though I was sitting right next to them all. Charlie didn't drop me off last that night, something I noticed and probably overthought. I wondered if he dropped me off before them so they could all discuss me. When I got home, my Dad was sitting in the living room watching TV; I could tell he was on edge about something as he didn't seem himself. I worried that he now felt uncomfortable around me—but that wasn't the issue.

"Where's Mum?" I asked, listening out for her presence in the kitchen or possibly upstairs.

"She's been arrested", He said softly.

We knew it was likely to happen, but it didn't stop me from feeling any less guilty about it. I knew that my Sarah's Mum would press charges. I knew they wouldn't just accept she had been punished for her actions and leave it, my Mum had assaulted her and it was illegal. Was she going to go to prison? Was my Mum going to spend time in prison because I couldn't handle what was said to me? This was all my fault! My Dad explained that the police who came to speak to her had been really nice and friendly, and they didn't treat Mum harshly. They asked her to come down to the police station with them so she could give her statement. What if she never got out? But after a few hours that seemed much longer, my Dad received a phone call from her asking him to come and collect her. Of course, I went with him to get her from that place. I couldn't wait to see her again and hug her; she was going through this because of me. She was really shaken up when we finally got to her, she was standing outside the police station on her own and I could tell the ordeal had scared her. Fortunately, something in Sarah's Mum statement was deemed invalid and so they couldn't accept her statement therefore, my Mum was released on a caution. I regularly checked all of Sarah's family's social media for days afterwards. Status from her Dad read, "it's great knowing what you can get away with, it's great to know". This was a threat that he wanted us to see and a threat that I lived in fear of for a very long time.

After so many days of waiting for Sarah to get in contact with me, to ask how I was feeling, I had lost hope. She clearly did not care about me the way I did her and that was ok. She was angry with my family and me and I would let her deal with that her way. Our friendship had come to an end once again. But due to this whole experience, my friendship with others grew. Olivia completely disagreed with how Sarah's Mum had acted and was absolutely sickened by the consequences. She reached out that she was there for me from now on, and we've become incredibly close friends ever since.

Due to my suicide attempt, I had to attend a meeting with a psychiatric doctor the following week to discuss a plan to help me get better, so I didn't attempt to take my own life again. They asked me, "Do you regret your actions now?" I answered yes, but I knew the real answer was no, but I couldn't say no because I knew this wasn't what everyone in the room wanted to hear. They increased my dosage of medication and arranged a triage appointment for counselling sessions for the following week. I was going back to therapy, and more medication was coming my way. I was being safely monitored, so they would only give me a week's supply of medication each time as they wouldn't risk them being used in an attempt to overdose again. My Mum attended all my doctor's appointments with me. She had done so ever since the doctor had touched me when I was younger, so she attended the triage appointment for counselling with me. When the nurse at my triage appointment condemned me for needing my Mum present, in her own words, "it's time for you to grow up now and stop needing Mum here", I felt an instant panic and could feel myself getting stressed out and worked up. I thought they were going to ask my Mum to leave me but she wouldn't because she knew I didn't want her to. The nurse asked me some questions, and when she asked, "Have you attempted suicide in the last 48 hours?" or something along those lines (stupid question! someone doesn't read their medical notes properly), I answered truthfully and said, "Yes". She quickly grabbed her office telephone and dialled a number and waited for it to connect. I had no clue what was happening. When someone answered on the opposite end, she started the sentence with "I need a section…" and added a list of numbers—I know now this only meant I was to be put on the emergency list for counselling, but at the time I panicked I was about to be sectioned for trying to take my own life, I turned to my Mum like a deer in headlights and her expression matched mine. We both thought at any moment two men were going to come in and take me away without choice and against our will. When we finally left the appointment, my Mum was absolutely disgusted with how I had been treated by the nurse and put in an official complaint about her behaviour. Thankfully it wasn't a shock to them as there had been complaints from others about her lack of sympathy and sensitivity. She definitely didn't have the right personality for the job and the wrong attitude for working with anyone with mental health issues, never mind a young person with mental health issues who had just attempted to take their own life. I said to my Mum, "if that's what people are greeted with when they come here to ask for help, no wonder people stop asking".

In my opinion, the counselling service I was provided after the suicide attempt wasn't very good or successful. I didn't build a very good rapport with the selected therapist and he didn't seem to understand me or any of my problems. My Mum was present for these sessions as I still didn't feel comfortable without her there. The therapist repeatedly would say statements like, "nobody can stop you, Josh, if you want to be a doctor, nobody can stand in your way". He was providing me with positive affirmations, but I knew nobody could stand in my way. Lack of determination and career goals weren't my problem, the issue was I didn't want to wake up each morning, but he just didn't seem to understand that. After the allocated six sessions were completed, the counselling sessions came to an end, and I was relieved when they did. My scores on the depression quiz, which was asked and filled in each week, didn't really alter that much, and only a month later, I stopped taking my medication.

If there was one good thing to come out of the overdose attempt, it made me realise how quickly my life could be over. I realised that the choice to live was mine. One minute I could be here, and the next I could be gone. So I decided that if I continued living, I wanted to do everything I could to try and be happy. This meant I had to admit all of this to someone who had become incredibly important to me.

CHAPTER SEVEN

When you have gone through something as brutal as a suicide attempt, when you've been moments away from no longer being here with your family, your friends and all your loved ones, you can't help but put life into perspective, even if it had been self-inflicted. For me, I knew what I wanted, and I no longer cared what people thought about it. But the history behind this decision needs to be explained to you first.

A year previous to the suicide attempt, around the time I started to be unfaithful to Sarah, I downloaded a dating app that I had been told about by a colleague from work. He explained that it was an app of gay men who live in the area, and you could speak to them on there and possibly arrange to meet up if that's what you wanted. It stuck in my mind when he said that there were many 'in the closet' men on there pretending to be straight. I think I resonated with that as I started to question my own sexuality. Looking back, I think I knew what was happening. There were hints, some subtle hints and some not so subtle. My Mum always tells the story of when I was younger, we all sat with the Argos catalogues writing our list of Christmas presents, when an advert came on the television for a princess fairy castle. She said my head shot up, and I was in complete awe of it. Instead, she bought me the new Action Man army camp, a present that found itself still in its plastic wrapping hidden away weeks later. I remember watching 'Harry Potter And The Goblet of Fire' and understanding exactly why the girls would fancy the character Cedric Diggory and of course, there aren't many straight males that can say they knew the choreography to 'I'm A Slave 4 U' by Britney Spears at the age of 7 or 8 years old. However, I had denied it to other people for so long that I denied it to myself too. I want to make it very clear that up until that year, I had never even contemplated a relationship with another man, even if I had moments of experimenting. This one night, when I downloaded the dating app, I logged on hoping to speak to someone else like me, someone who wasn't quite sure who or what they were, someone who would understand me and someone I could relate to. After a few failed conversations with others, I found him. This one profile stood out and we talked for a few days, sometimes he'd ignore my message and I'd find myself really annoyed and delete the app. Usually, when I had logged back on, he would have replied or started a new conversation. Eventually, he sent me a picture of himself and asked for one in return. Shamefully I sent him a picture that wasn't myself. It was of another boy. I believed he would lose interest straight away once he saw the real me. I admit I did become a little obsessed with this profile; I wanted him to want me, I needed him to want me, and eventually, he did.

The first time we met was a night when my parents were away on holiday and both my brothers had gone to the same music festival. When he asked me to meet him, I knew I would be able to without being questioned by my family about where I was going. He asked me to meet him, but he wanted to meet in the area close to where Sarah's Dad lived and the last thing I wanted was to have my car spotted. It would ruin everything. Instead, we chose to meet in an industrial area not too far from where I lived. I remember pulling up in my little silver Renault Clio in front of his white Audi A4. There were a few moments of waiting and eventually, he flicked the light inside his car so I could see it was really him. Luckily it was really him, so I got out of my car and walked over to get into his. The moment before I opened the passenger door, I dramatically thought in my head, "I'm going to die". I panicked that he could possibly rape me, kill me and hide my body. My parents would come back from their holiday to my brothers telling them I had gone missing and they'd have no idea where to even start looking for me—I'm sure you are aware by now I'm an over-thinker. Fortunately, he didn't kill me.

He held out his hand in an awkward hand position, his elbow rested on the armrest and he wanted me to clasp his hand and shake it, but I had no idea what he wanted me to do until he said, "you're supposed to shake my hand", we both laughed awkwardly, he simply said, "you alright?" At that moment I knew I liked him a lot. He has this tone to his voice, it's warm, kind and friendly, and from his voice and smile, I knew he would be a nice genuine person. We talked for a little while about feeling the way we did about ourselves and how we both didn't want anyone to find out this side to us and then we arrived at a small secluded car park to be more private. He asked me if the rather explicit picture I had previously sent him was really mine (sorry to our families reading this) and then we overstepped the line of strangers or friends to something more. But the car park wasn't as private as we planned, and a car's headlights lit up the darkness. I immediately ducked down so I wouldn't be seen or recognised. I volunteered that we could go back to my house knowing that it was free, he seemed really hesitant at first, but it was probably safer than finding another secluded car park and potentially being disturbed again. We went straight upstairs, ignoring the dogs barking from the kitchen door (Jasper, my Nan's dog Megan and their son Oscar), but as we approached my bedroom door, I suddenly remembered there were pictures of Sarah and me all over my bedroom, and he was about to see them. What if he knew her? What if he would tell her? Or tell someone who would tell her? Obviously, I didn't think he would tell her because he didn't want anyone to know about him either. As he was leaving the bedroom, he started to look at the pictures of Sarah and me. "This your girlfriend?" He went on to then ask where she was from. They were from the same area and I became more suspicious that he recognised her. It turned out his sister went to the same dance classes as Sarah, his sister being the girl who would throw me out of the nightclub for making Sarah cry the next year. I admit I should have felt guilty that I had been unfaithful, but in all honesty, at that moment, I did not. The guilt came later. He dropped me back off to pick my own car up from the industrial estate. I asked him what he did for a living on the way back. He told me that he worked as an admin, but this turned out to be a lie to protect himself from me finding out who he really was. I chose not to hide the truth from him. I told him I was a barber and a student, he admitted to recognising me from when I worked in the nightclub. As I drove myself back home, I questioned whether he was going to want to see me again.

I don't remember how long it was until when we next met up, but I do remember he was the one who instigated seeing one another again. Unfortunately, I didn't have a free house this time, so I had to drive to the industrial estate again and he took me to a very quiet country road. It was tucked away and in complete darkness. This soon became our regular spot, but soon we weren't just enjoying each other bodies, we were talking in-depth to each other and getting to know each other. He finally told me his name was Mike and showed me pictures of his family, that was when I recognised his sister, Natalie and I showed him mine too, he recognised my future sister-in-law Rachael, who I am extremely close to. This secret meet up place was unfortunately ruined by the local farmer who lived up the road. He pulled up in a van with a huge bright light on the back that lit up the whole of my car. Mike had no choice but to climb into the front completely naked and drive my car away as the farmer shouted, "WE ARE VIDEOING YOU! GET OFF THE LAND!" We swore on the way back we would never do this again; we swore we were going to stop seeing one another as it was becoming too risky that people would find out about us. But we didn't stop. With fewer and fewer choices of places to meet one another, I had to build the courage to go to the spot he originally suggested the first time we met. Even though it was very risky, we went in his car to avoid being spotted. This then became our place. I still drive past here on a regular basis to this day, and every time, I think of the conversations and passionate moments we had together there.

Only a few months after we first met, Mike invited me to spend Bonfire Night with him. He wanted to drive up to Rivington Pike, part of the West Pennine Moors, to watch the fireworks from the town below in the car. I remember him taking a wrong turn and driving onto a brick slabbed road that led to a dead end. He reversed off, but he was mounting the bricks backwards and I could see he was getting stressed out that the bricks were going to damage his car. I stayed completely silent, not wanting him to get even more stressed, eventually he managed to make his way out the turn and found a lay-by hillside view of the town below. We watched the fireworks and talked and talked. He pulled me into him so we could have a cuddle, something so simple that we hadn't done together. I rested my head against his chest, listening to his heartbeat, something I still enjoy doing. He placed his chin against the top of my head and he whispered into my ear, "I like you". I knew what he meant, he had feelings for me, but he couldn't do that. He wasn't allowed to do that. He knew I was still with Sarah, but by this point, I knew the relationship with her was coming to an end, but that didn't mean I was ending my relationship with her to start one with him. We didn't plan on getting feelings for one another. I couldn't say it back to him that night and I did my best to avoid him for a little while after that. I was terrified of what was happening because I knew I liked him too.

I was at work one day on the business social media page. The boss had followed a profile for a well-known band in the area to help get some promotion for the salon. I decided to do some research into some other bands in the area to help branch the business out there. I came across an acoustic duo named '10th Fret', and there he was, Mike. He was part of this duo. He'd never even told me that he was a singer. I texted him asking about it, and we arranged to meet up again that night on a little country road near a motorway bridge. He wanted to know how I had found out and innocently asked if he ever got somewhere with his music career to never sell a story on him. Bless him.

Then going into 2015, I had ended my relationship with Sarah and by this part of the book, you will already know all the drama and events that have happened since, but behind the scenes of the drama with her and the potential new relationship with Jodie, I was meeting up with Mike too. I ended the complicated relationship with Mike several times during 2015. He usually would demand that we had the conversation face-to-face. I knew it was hurting him, and it was hurting me too, but I knew at that point I couldn't give him what he wanted from me. But he'd always convince me he was happy with whatever decision I made, as long as it meant we could still see each other.

We carried on secretly meeting up with one another and were almost caught a few times. We arranged to meet back at Rivington; he was on his way back from playing at a gig, so we decided to meet there separately. My friends had become suspicious when I said I had plans and not long after leaving the estate where I lived, I noticed they were following me. I remember trying to lose them for a while, but they were persistent. They rang me laughing and said, "Who's the girl you are going to meet?" I would lie and tell them it was just a random girl from a dating app, but that made them want to follow me more. It became dangerous trying to lose them at one point, but eventually, they gave up and I got to spend some time with Mike without being disturbed or spotted by them.

Mike decided it would be safer for us to meet in hotels instead of outside in cars, so to save us being caught together, he would book a room in local hotels and we would stay over. I would tell my parents that I was going out drinking with my friends and staying over at their houses, and I would then tell my friends I was staying at home, going to a girl's house, or going to a party. The first time we met in a hotel was a disaster. He went in first to check in and went to the room and then texted me the room number so I could quickly walk in trying not to be spotted, trying to stay less suspicious. He asked me to bring my barbering tools so I could cut his hair while I was there. However, the hotel staff were probably more than aware of what was going on. I rushed to the room and knocked on the door, but nobody answered. I knocked again, no answer. I rang him, getting stressed, waiting outside this hotel room and after some debate over the room number, we realised I had gone to the completely wrong hotel. I am so thankful that nobody had accommodated the room that night. I honestly loved our hotel trips. He would buy some snacks and drinks, usually a bottle of wine or beer (this was before he knew I didn't like wine or beer). He bought a bottle of Dandelion and Burdock once, which in my opinion, is the worst flavour in existence. During one of our hotel stays, I walked in with my barbering tools again, trying to look less suspicious and bumped into a girl I vaguely knew, she was working at the hotel and I had no idea. She asked what I was doing there, and luckily the bag of barbering tools made my story believable, I hoped. But the more the hotel trips happened, the more I knew Mike was getting strong feelings for me, and I didn't want him to, even though I knew I was getting feelings for him too.

Mike started to come to the shop I worked in for his haircut, but I think it was just an excuse to see me. He even pretended to use the sunbeds upstairs just so we could talk for 5 minutes before he went on. I started to get brutal in ending our relationship over text and insisting he left me alone, but he never did, he wouldn't listen and he would come weekly just to say hello and although it was frustrating, I loved that he did. He wanted me. I enjoyed my time when I was around him. It definitely helped that he was a really good-looking boy and his Edward Cullen style quiff, but there was more to Mike. It was the way he was with me, the way he seemed to care about me differently than anyone else ever had before. Just before the "secret affair" with Charlie began, I called things off with Mike and explained I needed some time to myself, and he had to respect that and this time, he did. We didn't see each other that much over these months, but he would text every now and then to see how I was doing, but our relationship together seemed like it had been put to bed. But for me, my head had begun to spiral, not only had I started a form of relationship with Mike for the past ten months, but now I had a "secret affair" with Charlie too, I knew then what I couldn't deny to myself any longer, I was gay. But I refused to say the words aloud and I never told Charlie about Mike. He only knew that I had a friend called Mike who was in a band.

This now brings us to waking up from the overdose. I knew from the moment I was home that day that I wanted to see Mike. Since I had last seen him, it had been a month or so, but I knew I could feel happy around him. I felt comfortable with him; I didn't have to put on a show or compete with anyone else for his affection. I knew how much he liked me and that he could make me happy again. Mike was like a comfort blanket for me. He'd become the safety net in my life without me even releasing. He wanted what was best for me. He had encouraged me to sign up for university but also encouraged me when I said I didn't want to be there anymore. When everything was feeling disconnected and strange, I knew he could be the one person I could sit with, talk to and feel like I wasn't the "weird" one. But if he wanted us to become something solid, he needed to know what had happened. He had to know what he was taking on board and if that's what he really wanted.

I was basically put under house arrest returning home from the hospital due to the suicide attempt, so it wasn't as easy to leave the house without being questioned on where I was going or my parents checking to see if a friend's car was waiting for me outside. I had to stage a phone call with my friend James to pick me up from the petrol station across the field from where we lived, but in reality, Mike was at the petrol station waiting for me. I ran across the field as quickly as I could and got into his car the second he pulled into me. I was absolutely terrified that my Mum and Dad would be checking on me or sending my brother to make sure I was honest. I wasn't. We drove to our usual spot, the original country road, and we talked a lot. Our conversations had come such a long way from the beginning of our time together. We'd gone from arranging that we would both get girlfriends, both get married, have our own children and we'd just pretend to be best friends. We'd continue our affair by sitting in the car talking about a possible exclusive relationship in the future. Looking back now, the original plan for us was a ridiculously bad idea and would have potentially hurt a lot of people, but it seemed to be our only option at the time. But this night and leading up to this night, Mike had made it clear he wanted to be more, he wanted to be together, just not publicly— neither of us was ready for that yet. He'd just come back from a holiday with his friends and looked really tanned and he looked good. He admitted that he had "pulled" on holiday and I felt incredibly jealous. I had no right to, but I did. I told him about what had happened over the past few months with Charlie and why it had stopped and he was jealous of that. We decided in that conversation that we would be exclusive to each other from that point onwards. There would be no more being open and sleeping around with other people. But I knew that he needed to know about what had happened only days before. I unloaded everything, starting with something along the lines of "You say you want to get with me, but you don't know what you're getting with…" before waffling on about my addiction to self-harming, my depression, my anxiety, my suicide attempt and everything that could possibly put a person off me. I hoped in a way that it would scare him off, I thought that it would be easier to get all the pain and heartbreak done in one week, but he turned and looked at me with the most compassionate facial expression and said, "I don't care, I like you". He went on to explain that he'd already seen my scars and cuts on my arms during our times together, but he was waiting for me to talk to him about it, he knew all about my low moods and when I was feeling down, he knew that whenever I would text him telling him, we should stop seeing each other that I was struggling and would wait until I was ready to start seeing him again. This whole time, he completely understood me when I didn't even understand myself. He understood me even though he couldn't relate to me and he wasn't judging me. In 2018, Taylor Swift released the song 'Delicate', and the lyrics go, "This ain't for the best, my reputation's never been worse, so you must like me for me…". Every time I hear those lyrics, I'm taken back to how I felt at that moment when Mike said, "I don't care, I like you". My world was falling apart around me and I had someone telling me they didn't care about all that, and he still liked me. We now say that was the official start of our relationship, but we didn't identify as each other's boyfriends for a while. I remember, we went on our first official date to Nando's, we went to one a drive away, so we were less likely to be spotted, on the way home, I asked him what he saw us as, "are we together?", he replied with "Yeah, seems that way". I asked, "So you're my boyfriend?" The word felt completely alien on my tongue. I could sense his uncomfortableness with the word too. He told me, "I don't really like that term. You can be my PP". I looked at him confused, waiting for further explanation, "penis partner", he laughed. That's been an inside joke between us ever since. That trip to Nando's was nerve-wracking for us both. Mike had never really been in a relationship before and this showed in his behaviour. I watched as he eyed up the blonde-haired and tanned waitress who served us, so I asked the question with a raised eyebrow. "You like her?" He absentmindedly, to my sarcasm, responded with, "Yeah, she's my type her." We went to a restaurant in the Trafford Centre. As he put his phone on the table, a notification from a dating app popped up, he looked at me alarmed and I expressed my annoyance at that. He claimed he just hadn't gotten around to deleting it, but I knew he just wasn't ready to let go of that side of his life yet. His friends, his family and everyone else in his life had no idea about me. I thought nobody on my side knew about him, but my Mum was already clued up and aware as to what was happening.

He had been coming around to our house bringing his guitar as a disguise as to why he was really there, pretending to be writing music together but instead we were watching films and enjoying each other—sorry to the family again! We thought we were pulling the wool over everybody's eyes; we thought we were being so clever about sneaking around until one day, I was pulled aside by my Mum. Mike was staying over in a hotel for his work's Christmas do. He wanted me to wait in the hotel room for him to get back. I packed my laptop so I had something to do whilst waiting and some clothes to stay over. The cover story to my family was I was going doing a gig with Mike, and we would be staying over, but as I got my laptop charger out of the spare living room, my Mum came in behind me to talk

"I know, sweetheart," she said, with her eyes filling up with tears.

"You know what?" I was actually confused about what she was talking about.

"I know what's going on".

"What's going on?" Did she know? How could she know? Surely not!

"I know about Mike,"

"What about him?" No, please, no! She can't know! She isn't meant to know! "I know you're together," she whispered.

"Don't be daft. He's my best mate." I tried to laugh it off. That was my last attempt at keeping this part of my life a secret. Once I admitted this, that would be it, the lid would be off the jar and it could never go back on.

"Darling, I'm your Mum, I know."

My eyes filled up too and I admitted defeat to her. Of course, she knew, she would always know, it's just a Mum thing, isn't it? They know even when they don't.

"Ok, but you can't tell anyone, not even Dad."

"We'll tell him when you are ready to." She hugged me so tightly and kissed my forehead. I could hear the emotion in her voice as she said, "Have a nice night".

Shit! This was not the plan! We had only been exclusive for two months and we had not even spoken about telling people about our relationship yet. Nobody was meant to find out yet. What was he going to say? Do I even tell him? How could I not? This wasn't just my secret, it was his secret too and he had every right to know. I arrived at the hotel and met him in the hotel room. As soon as I put my things in, the words came out of me like vomit, "I need to tell you about something." He looked at me, alarmed and slightly confused but didn't ask any questions, "My Mum knows. She pulled me as I was leaving and told me she knows, I couldn't get out of it" I waffled on explaining how she could potentially know, he interrupted me and asked, "Did you admit to her?" I nodded, knowing he would be disappointed in me, "but don't worry. She won't tell anyone. She promised she wouldn't." He didn't say another word, he walked into the bathroom, closed the door and the next minute there was a scream of frustration, anger and pain all in the same breath and I realised at that moment that was exactly how I felt too, I wanted to scream it out and then get on with whatever had happened. That was exactly what he did. He came out of the bathroom completely composed and returned to his usual laid back self, and said, "Ok, I'm fine. I'm going to go back downstairs. I'll come back in an hour or so, you ok?" I nodded and set my laptop on the bed to watch a series whilst I waited for him, hoping something would distract me from feeling everything I was feeling at that moment. I knew he was angry deep down with me, but I'm so glad now that my Mum pulled me aside that day and said those words because that was the pivotal point in our relationship, that was the moment we accepted that people were going to find out about us eventually, but we liked each other enough to be ok with that.

    The following week, as Mike stood up, getting ready to leave to say goodbye, I was following behind him when he turned around on the spot, stopping me in my tracks and kissed me. It seemed completely random, but then for the first time, he said the words, "I love you". He waited a few seconds for me to say it back, but I couldn't. It wasn't that I didn't believe him, but I don't think he truly knew how powerful those words could be to someone and for me, I would only say the words when I knew I truly meant them, and at that point, I was still hurting and still not feeling secure in my life. After an awkward laugh from us both, he smiled and said "It's ok", and then he left to return home, to his family who didn't know where he had been all night. Don't worry, I did say the words eventually, but he had to wait until there was no doubt about them and it took a trying time for me to be sure.

CHAPTER EIGHT

Although my relationship with Mike was truly beginning, my friendship with my group of friends was slowly distancing. After my overdose, I felt like my friends began to see me as unstable and unpredictable and in a way, they were completely accurate. I had started to take my prescribed Sertraline again, but this time my friends, due to the overdose, were aware of my mental health issues and the medication I was taking. It was more ideal that they were aware, as we had just booked a holiday to Prague together. It was meant to be an amazing holiday. It was my first 'lad's holiday', and it felt like I finally had everything I had wanted when I was in school with this group of lads, just to be accepted into the group. But it seemed this holiday was the cracking of the glass for our friendship, as I started to lose control of my emotions again.

I was more than excited to be going away, jokes were being made about how long I would last due to my 24 hours visit to Ibiza earlier in the year, but I knew I would be ok going away with my friends. We all stayed over at James' house the night before, they all played Fifa and I just watched them, we all really had a laugh that night. I forgot about the anxiety that I had of flying and it really hit me like a tonne of bricks whilst we were in the airport. I felt myself shaking and eventually had to go to the toilets to calm myself down, worried that my friends would notice I wasn't quite acting right. Charlie and James told me that my Mum had asked them to keep an eye on me during the holiday. It was understandable with the overdose, the Ibiza scenario and the whole year in general, she had become extremely worried about her not being there if I needed her. The way Charlie said it though, with an eye roll, made it appear as if he wasn't very keen on the idea of keeping an eye on me for her.

During the flight, I sat next to James. The other three were sitting together across the aisle from me. I had fallen asleep watching a film with my headphones in and as I woke up, the film had finished. I could only just hear the three friends talking and their topic of the conversation was me. One of the lads was saying to the other two, "this holiday would be perfect if Josh weren't there". At this point, I opened my eyes and felt the instant feeling of dread in my stomach. As this friend wished I wasn't here, Charlie laughed and whispered to him, "he's right there," trying to get him to be quiet, but the friend responded with, "I'd say it to him". He didn't need to say it again, he had already said it, and I'd heard him. Instantly I didn't want to be there. I was on a flight on the way to Budapest and all I wanted to do was go back home, but I couldn't do what I did with Ibiza again. I would just be laughed at all over again. I texted James sitting next to me about the conversation I had heard and he reassured me if anything was said to him, he would let me know. Stupidly, I left my iPad on the plane. I got that embarrassed and anxious when I forgot it; I just pretended I wasn't bothered about it, but my family got in touch with the airline and arranged for me to collect it upon returning to the airport.

Our rooftop apartment was absolutely amazing. It had one huge bedroom with four single beds and one other bedroom with a double bed. Charlie insisted that he wanted the double bed to himself, and even though we all find it bizarre and slightly annoying, we all just accepted and took the single beds in the room together. One friend had even suggested that Charlie could join us all in one room, but he insisted on having his own room because he was in a relationship with his Jodie now. This wasn't the only time he acted strangely during this holiday. One night in a nightclub, he was crouched down in the corner of the dance floor texting Jodie on his phone instead of being with us. I wasn't the only one who noticed it, luckily, and his strange behaviour became a topic of conversation. He wasn't being abnormal all the time, though, throughout the holiday, he was sometimes his usual hilarious self, playing pranks on some of us. We went on

Segway tours—something I was awful at, although not like one friend who fell off and injured his back—we joined an awful haunted house tour, but halfway through we made a run for it in the rain, we visited a strip club and drank all day and night. The night we visited the strip club, they forced me into having a lap dance, with the reason being I hadn't gone on holiday to Zante with them the previous year and they all had had one there. I went into the back room with the dancer and even with her incredible dancing skills, she noticed I wasn't getting aroused. I think by that point I knew what I preferred. Later that same night, Charlie pulled me to one side in a nightclub and asked me point blank, "Are you seeing someone?"

I played naive to his question and asked back, "What makes you say that?"

"You aren't yourself. You don't seem interested in anyone".

He had worked out that I wasn't single anymore, but he could tell with my behaviour that I was faithful to someone back home. And this seemed to irritate him. In all honesty, I loved that, so I went further with the conversation to wind him up.

"So what if I was? You don't care, right?"

"Let me ask you this, is it a girl or a lad?"

"I can't say". I couldn't answer that without giving too much information away. They all knew I was spending a lot of time with Mike and I didn't want to give his secret away to anyone, especially not Charlie.

"I don't mind if it's a girl, but it better not be a lad."

His comment frustrated me and I started to feel myself getting really angry with him. How dare he tell me how to live my life after what he'd done to me! He'd broken my heart, used me, guilt-tripped me into keeping his secret and now was trying to tell me I wasn't allowed to move on and be happy without him. Did he not want me to be happy? Did he want me to stay sad and depressed? Maybe he did. After all, I wouldn't be a threat to his new perfect relationship if I wasn't here anymore.

"You don't care. You said that." I replied and that was the conversation over. I got stupidly drunk that night and was violently sick in the apartment. As I lay down in the living room, I repeatedly said over and over, "You don't care so don't pretend to", they videoed me saying this. Without the background knowledge, the video seems bizarre and completely random, but when I watched it back, I knew exactly what was going through my head, and so did he, but it was much easier for him to make me look like the strange one.

The next night was our last night in Prague; I'd decided not to drink as much and try to keep a cool head. I may not have drunk as much as the night before, but I definitely did not keep a cool head. When we got back to the apartment, all of us were drunk and talking in various rooms. I was talking to Charlie on the bed in his room. He asked me if I wanted to stay in his room that night with him, but I declined. I still wasn't speaking to him properly, but I wasn't going to make a scene about it on the holiday in front of everyone. He brought up the suspicion of my relationship once again, but luckily, we were interrupted by one of our other friends as he came into the room and asked if he could stay in there with him. Charlie turned to everyone and made out that both me and the other friend were trying to stop in his room when he just wanted it for himself. He claimed to "refuse" both of our requests, although I had never requested it in the first place and asked us both to leave his room. I got in my own bed and whilst everyone was sleeping ready for the last day and to return back home, I got a text from him that said: "No more box"—that was officially the end of our secret affair. The fate of our friendship was left hanging on by a thread.

We spent our last day in a restaurant struggling to eat and chose to instead sleep off our hangovers—I remember being so tired that I tried to pay for my half of the bill with the wrong currency. When we arrived at the airport, I had to go to a phonebook to ring through to the lost and found department. I could barely hear them in the busy airport and was straining to make out what the person on the other end of the phone was saying. As I looked over at my friends, some of them were mimicking and doing impressions of me being on the phone. The feeling was back, the feeling of dread. Flashbacks of being taking the piss out of during my school years, people doing impressions of me and the boys in the street calling the way I walked all come flooding back to me in seconds. I felt completely uncomfortable. The iPad was finally returned to me and we were on our way to leave Prague and by this point, I just wanted to get home and be away from them. I don't think I said very much on the flight home. None of us did. We all continued to sleep off our hangovers.

Once we arrived back home, it was obvious that the friendship group dynamic had certainly changed. Charlie and one of our friends who hadn't come to Prague with us, the one I had confided in months previously, had clearly missed one another. He was Charlie's new favourite, he was now the one to be picked up first and dropped off last. On one occasion, one of the other lads in the group rang me to let me know that they were all in the pub in town and asked if I wanted to meet them. Nobody had let me know the plans previously, nobody had asked if I needed a lift there and nobody except this one friend had even thought to ring me and ask. I met them all at the pub, sitting on the end of the bench as they carried on watching the football and they hardly said one word to me. I can't remember how it happened, but the conversation turned to talking about our manly parts and without even thinking, I made a stupid comment about Charlie's parts in front of everybody. The comment was something like, "well, yours isn't exactly small", he saw a moment to embarrass me, a moment to humiliate me and he asked, "how would you know?" He looked at me with a smug look on his face. They all were looking at me, waiting for my answer. I had to think of something quick. I couldn't say "because I've seen it far too many times up close and personal" and he knew that, so I just had to say that his girlfriend, Jodie, had told me once.

Weeks later, during a night out pre-drinks, he confronted me again on the topic. He told me in front of everybody that he had spoken to Jodie about what I had said in the pub and that she denied any knowledge of ever talking about that to me. So once again, in front of everyone, he asked, "how would you know?" He had this smile on his face that almost looked thrilled at how uncomfortable and anxious I was feeling. It seemed he wanted to humiliate me, he wanted to put me under pressure and be embarrassed in front of all our friends, but most of all, he wanted me to look strange and weird because it suited the story he would tell them all at a later date. The same night, after a few too many drinks, I apologised to him for what happened between us. I told him I took full responsibility and I apologised for putting him in those awkward positions. The most bizarre thing was, he agreed. He agreed that it was all my fault and that I had seduced him and he took zero reasonability for what happened between us. I knew that I really had nothing to apologise for in my head and I knew I was being manipulated and controlled by him, but this was my last attempt at getting back to being his favourite. A conversation outside with his new favourite made it clear that I wasn't and that they had been speaking about me together. His new favourite told me that Charlie didn't like how I text him all day and all the time, he didn't like that I was trying too hard to impress him and that he didn't like me talking to Jodie about their relationship. It was very obvious why. He was scared that I would say something to her about us. After that conversation, I knew that the two of them had been talking about me being my back and that he was painting the scene of me being the strange and unstable one. After all, only months after an overdose, it wasn't exactly a hard picture to paint.

As Christmas approached, so did the annual nights out, and we all had a few planned. On Christmas Eve, we all went to the local pub. It was the place where everyone who had gone to our high school went on Christmas Eve, so everyone around us was people that we all knew, some people we liked and some people we didn't like so much. Sarah's cousin was also there that night. I was standing with some friends enjoying a drink when I caught her looking right at me, I looked back at her, and she said, "Josh, I really hate you."

"That's fine", I said with a slight smile, trying to keep the situation calm as the last thing I needed was more drama.

She continued to say how I had ruined her cousin's life and that she thought my Mum was disgusting for what she did. I, of course, defended my Mum and said she had every right to retaliate how she did that awful night, which turned up the intensity of the conversation. The cousin's friend got involved and began making threats about my Mum, saying, "I'm gonna smash her fucking face in when I see her". As I walked away to leave, saying bye to my friends, they shouted after "go on, go slit your wrist, you fucking freak", they were repeating what her aunt had said, what Sarah's Mum had said, they knew that those comments had affected me that much that I had attempted to take my own life. They were choosing to say them to me again (Years later, I had spoken to Sarah's cousin, and we have congratulated one another on how far we've both come and let the past be the past). As I got home, Charlie had rung my Mum to let her know what had gone on and apparently seemed worried about me. I was thrilled; he cared. He still cared about me after all the weeks it seemed that he didn't. Maybe I could become his favourite again? Even if we didn't ever rekindle our affair, I would be happy to be his good friend again instead of feeling like he didn't want me around. How wrong I was.

We all arranged to have a night out for Boxing Day. We went to a friends house for pre-drinks, the same friend's house where we had been secretly having sex months previously. I noticed he seemed to be staying away from me, avoiding me and that was fine. I left him to it until he pulled me to one side to have a conversation. He explained that he had only rung my Mum as he had promised her and it wasn't about being worried about me. He claimed he'd been informed on Christmas Eve night that I had been slating Jodie to people we knew and one person had told him about it (this person he claimed had told him had denied ever saying those words to him). I insisted I had never said that about Jodie and tried to make him see I got nothing out of making people we went to school with not like his girlfriend. I wouldn't achieve anything with that. Later the same night, he told me that he had decided he no longer wanted me to be friends with him. He said, "I will allow you to stay in the group, and allow these to speak to you, but I can't be your mate anymore." I tried to act completely fine with this decision and that it wasn't physically hurting me more than self-harming ever did. His last words to me were, "Do me a favour though, don't go killing yourself or anything stupid, I can't be arsed feeling guilty." I assured him, "I'll never kill myself over you." And that was it. The stupid secret affair was over and now our friendship was too. Could the friendship with the others stay the same if I was no longer allowed to be friends with the ringleader? How long would it last before they all turned their backs on me too? His new favourite told me the exact same thing the same night, telling me that he no longer wanted to be friends with me because he believed I had convinced my cousin to stop dating him, the reality was, I had wanted them to carry on dating because she was telling me everything that the two lads had been saying to each other about me, but she had decided she just didn't like him, there was no spark and instead of accepting that he just wasn't that much of a catch, he blamed me instead. In one night, two friends out of the group had made it very clear that they no longer wanted to be friends. I had two options, I either leave and go home or get absolutely bladdered. Initially, I tried to leave. I rang Mike and asked him if we could leave, but he was out drinking with his own friends in the same area so we could arouse suspicion by leaving, so instead, I returned inside and went straight for the bar to one of the other lads.

 The amount I drank that night broke a record for me. I had never been that drunk in my life before. I remember my friend and I were dancing on the dance floor when he asked me something about why I wasn't "pulling" and I just decided to admit that I had admitted to my Mum and my cousin, and I didn't see the point in lying anymore. So I confessed to him, "I'm with someone, yeah", he got excited and asked, "Who?" I replied, "I can't say because he doesn't want me to yet". But he knew who I meant straight away. He knew it was Mike. He was the only option. He pulled me to one side where it was quieter and so we could speak properly. He then asked me to be completely honest with him and admit if I had feelings or ever had feelings for Charlie. It was obvious everyone had been thinking this. Everyone was assuming that I was the one who had feelings, I was the gay one, I was the one who had "barked up the wrong tree", but it wasn't the wrong tree. In fact, the tree was just as "bent" as me, but he just wouldn't admit to them or himself. So I was completely honest with him. Would I have if I had been sober? Or if I had not had too much to drink? I'll never know now, but I do believe the amount I had drunk that night had a massive part to play in the fact I told him everything. I told him about the "secret affair".

He was shocked and in disbelief. But he did seem to believe me, and that was a start. The next day, I was driving around with my cousin when the friend rang me to confirm the story I had told him the night before, to see if whilst sober I was still standing by what I had said to him and I did. But I begged him to not do anything about it. I begged him not to say anything to anyone; I told him that my friendship with Charlie would never be sorted if he knew that I had said anything to him, so it was best that we all forgot about the "secret affair" and moved on.

The next night out together was New Year's Eve. I had decided days previously that I wasn't going to go out with them all. Mike's gig with his band had been cancelled, so we were talking about potentially spending the night together, chilling in his car and watching the fireworks again like we had done the year previous for Bonfire Night. But on the day, I decided I really wanted to sort things out with my friends. I wanted to make sure I stayed in this group, I couldn't be left alone, and if I started to miss nights out together, eventually I wouldn't be invited at all, and that fate seemed worse than death to me. I had willingly faced death, but I couldn't face losing any more people. It was evident during the night that my two former friends did not want to sort anything out with me, they didn't want me there and they made that clear by wishing everyone "Happy New Year" except for me. In the beer garden, I spotted Charlie talking to James' sister. She looked over at me and then he did and then they continued to talk to one another. It was evident they were talking about me. I have found out since he was telling her that I had made a move on him in Prague and that he had turned me down and that's why I had been acting strange since we've come back home and that he doesn't want to be around me anymore. It was the perfect story to cover up everything that had happened to us, but then he went on to say because of my medication that I was dangerous, twisted and deluded and that I had been making up strange lies, and he thought it was weird. He knew exactly how to turn people against me and it worked perfectly. That night, I stayed with the same friend that I had spent Boxing Night with and we both got horrendously drunk once again. He asked me some questions again about the "secret affair" and explained that he wanted to speak to Charlie about it, but I pleaded with him not to do this. I knew that this friend would be turned against me if he spoke about what I had told him, he was already disbelieving me, so it wouldn't take much to spin the story that I was a deluded depressive. We continued the night and met up with some friends who had come back from university. Before I knew what was happening, we were walking down an alleyway next to the club. That night was the very first time that I tried drugs. I was told it was cocaine, but my reaction to it I've found out since doesn't seem to be a typical reaction from cocaine, so I have no idea what it really was. Lesson learnt that night, do not take drugs at all, especially when you don't know what they are. My heart was pounding. I could hear it above everything else. It seemed like the music had stopped, but everyone was still dancing and my whole body was shaking. I headed for the toilets to try to compose myself but there was no luck, I really panicked and locked myself in the cubicle whilst I suffered a severe panic attack. I rang Mike and asked him to come and get me from the nightclub. I got in his car around the corner from the club and he quickly drove me away. He knew he couldn't take me home in that state, so we pulled up on a motorway bridge and talked about what had happened. I put my head in my hands, trying to stop my surroundings from spinning and as I looked up, Mike was fast asleep in the driver's seat and it was going light outside. I had been asleep for over an hour without even releasing. It was a new year. I waited for Mike to wake up as I reflected on what the last year had been like for me. I had gone into the year with a relationship with Sarah, but it was coming to an end. I had a group of friends I felt completely myself with. I was working at a busy salon and I thought I finally knew what happiness was, but in such a short time, I had lost it all. Sarah and her whole family hated me with a passion. Some even wished me dead. My friends were one by one turning against me, I was now working in an extremely quiet salon completely secluded and on my own in there and I thought I'd never be happy again. Mike was doing everything he could, but how happy could someone be when the relationship had to be kept completely secret.

Into the new year, my friends had started to plan another holiday together, they were discussing Tenerife, but I noticed that when I messaged back to say that I was up for it, that Charlie had blocked me from all his social media. I tried to text and ring him to sort out our friendship, but he had blocked my number too. He had removed all chance of me contacting him. We have never said a word to one another since. A few weeks after, I texted my friend, the one I had told everything to, I asked if he wanted to get some lunch, but he declined and told me that he was working that day. It was quite normal for us to turn up at each other's workplace, the lads would come into the salon I worked in, this friend worked at a supermarket and we had all been before whilst he was working so I drove down to say hello and have some reassurance that we were ok, hoping that he hadn't spoken to his friend about what had happened. But he wasn't there. His colleague told me he was off work that day. He had lied to me. In a desperate attempt in needing some reassurance, I drove around to his house, and he was there. I texted him again to test him, "How's workmate?", he replied "Busy". I knew then that another one had turned his back on me. Only James was still willing to talk to me and I knew that if my own friends wouldn't believe me, nobody would. On the way home, I shut everything off once again. I switched my emotions off as I couldn't deal with any more loss. A week before this, I had had my third tattoo, it was on my left forearm and it read "accomplished the struggle", the artist had spelt accomplished with only one "c". I suppose it was quite fitting, really, as the struggle hadn't been accomplished at all. The struggle was still ongoing and I was drowning in it.

I drove to the chemist and purchased some over the counter sleeping tablets. I went home and went straight to the kitchen medicine cupboard to get more sleeping tablets and some painkillers and stuffed them in my hoodie pocket. My Mum was home, so I had to be clever about it. If I had just gone upstairs, she would come to check on me, and I didn't want to be checked on, I wanted to be left alone long enough that I couldn't be saved this time. I explained to her that I was going to watch a television series I had been watching, had a nap and then went upstairs and swallowed the whole packet of the new sleeping tablets I had purchased, with some of my Mum's from the medicine cupboard, and a sleeve of painkillers too. I would have taken more, but I could already feel myself becoming drowsy, so I believed that I had done enough for it to work. I pulled the blinds down and lay back down on my bed in the dark. I closed my eyes and hoped they wouldn't open again. I woke up at one point with a gasp, I had heard my name being called, but it wasn't from my Mum or anyone else in the house. I drifted back off. Who had called my name? Some may not believe this, but I do. I think that I was visited by my sister Chelsey. I remember feeling a lot of pain, my legs, my arms, my head. The pain was very intense and completely uncomfortable. The next thing I remember was my Mum being on the bed with me, two male paramedics in the room at the bottom of the bed, my Dad and my brothers in the doorway and a female stood behind them. Her face caught my attention as she didn't look as stressed out and anxious as the other faces in the room. She simply looked curious. She had long dark auburn hair, freckles around her nose and similar features that my Mum once would have had when she was younger. Was this her? Was this my sister Chelsey? Had she come to take me away? As upsetting as it may seem, I was relieved, I thought it had been a success and I was finally leaving behind the pain. The next thing I remember is being in hospital, opening my eyes, my Dad and my Mum were on the right of me, my cousin and my Auntie were to my left. Facing me at the end of the bed with a smile as I opened my eyes was Mike. What was he doing here? I don't remember much after that.

    My Mum described this overdose as far more severe than the first and they thought that had been bad enough. Apparently, I was very lucky that my brother Adam found me when he did, as my oxygen levels were dangerously low, so I had to be placed on oxygen and my organs started to struggle to function properly so I had to be placed on a drip to clean them. My Mum had answered the phone to one of the many missed calls from Mike and had to explain to him what had happened and invited him to come to the hospital if he wanted to. He rang my cousin and collected her so they could come together. It didn't seem like it would be good news for a while, and the doctors wanted to keep me overnight to observe me. I remember my Dad's face as he watched me, his eyes were bright red and full of tears and I could tell he had been crying. They have all told me since that due to the damage to my brain from the medication, I was talking nonsense and slurring questions to my cousin, asking her, "Do you still have your horse? Have you fed it?"—she doesn't own a horse. I asked my Mum about her university degree (when she never went to university) and I kept frowning at Mike jokingly. It's something we've all laughed about since, making jokes about the rubbish that I said and the way I was speaking but the reality as I was damaged. My speech was slurred and my brain wasn't forming sentences or grasping reality together properly. My Dad thought that I was going to be brain-damaged. I woke up halfway through the night and panicked about being in a hospital. This was the first time I'd stayed over in a hospital since the assault, and in panic, my eyes were looking for my Mum, but my body couldn't move. She must have sensed my panic and placed her warm hand on my arm. I could feel her touch, but I couldn't bring my own hand to meet hers, but I felt safer knowing she was there with me and drifted back off to sleep. I woke up to the elderly man who was in the bed across from me throughout the night, passed away. His curtains had been pulled so the nurses could care for his body. I remember struggling to have the strength to whisper to my Mum asking her, "Has he died?" She nodded silently and at that moment, I felt jealous of him. I felt jealous that he had died. Some may find this disgusting, I do myself, this man may have wanted to continue his life, he may have been fighting with every breath he had to stay alive and there I was willingly trying to stop myself from ever breathing again, but I did not want to be alive anymore, the pain I felt was just too much for me to handle. I woke up again needing to use the toilet and asked my Mum if she could take me. The walk was incredibly painful and slow, my legs didn't seem to work properly, and I couldn't pick my feet up, so I walked with my toes curled over or on the side of my feet. I woke the next day with bruises all over my feet from the way I had been walking. I had a meeting with a psychiatric team the next morning and they expressed their concern that I had attempted to take my own life twice in less than six months. They repeatedly asked me, "Do you regret what you did?" I replied honestly and said "No". They then asked, "Do you plan on attempting to take your own life again?" I replied honestly and said, "Yes." In my head, I was already planning how I would do it next time, how I could make sure it worked the next time. I concluded that overdoses weren't working for me, so I planned on hanging myself next time. Surely that had to work. They arranged more meetings with a psychiatrist to discuss further medication and I was placed on the emergency list for more counselling. They expressed more concern about my weight. At that point, I was weighing around six stone or less, so they prescribed me Mirtazapine as an antidepressant, anti-anxiety and relaxant. Over the weeks, after repeatedly filling in the depression questionnaire with my psychiatrist, I was placed on the strongest dosage of Mirtazapine they could allow, and they informed me that if I was to need a stronger dosage, that it would require me being in 24-hour surveillance and if I also attempted to overdose within a short period of time again that I would be sectioned to this 24-hour surveillance without choice.

When I got home, the atmosphere was far worse than the first overdose. This time there was anger here too. My brother, Adam was extremely angry with me, he was furious at the consequences that my actions were having on our parents and I think he saw me as being selfish, and he was completely right. Suicide is a incredibly selfish act, the pain you feel isn't wiped away, it is simply passed on to your loved ones left behind, but at that point, I just didn't care that it was.

CHAPTER NINE

After the second suicide attempt and speaking to my therapist at the time, I decided I needed to delete and block all the remaining friends from the group of friends I had, minus James and one other. I had a lot of developed pictures of memories with these friends stuck up on my bedroom wall, so during work one day, I asked my Mum to remove all the pictures and get rid of them. The next day, I started to tear off the wallpaper in my bedroom and suggested to my Mum that I should redecorate the room as I wanted a fresh start. It wasn't just about ripping wallpaper down and putting fresh paint on the walls. I really needed this fresh start and with all my friends now gone, it was the perfect time to move on with my life. I never really did that though, that previous year is something I have struggled with ever since. What would I do if I saw those friends now? I would say hello and be civil, but if I could say what I really wanted to say, I would thank you for showing me a difference between the kind of friends I wanted and the kind of friends I needed. To the real Charlie, I thank you so much. If it wasn't for you, I don't think I would accept myself as gay and because the way we were together and all the time we spent together privately helped me accept that I could be in a relationship with a boy and not feel strange about it. So if you are reading this, which I highly doubt if you were, you wouldn't make it to this part without throwing the book away anyway but thank you for helping me see who I was and what I need and I hope one day you accept who you are too.

One good thing that came out of the overdose was that my Dad got to meet Mike properly. After he had arrived with my cousin, Mike said that my Dad shook his hand and they all stood around my bedside hoping and praying that I would pull through this critical phase. Once I was back home and settled, my Mum asked if I would give permission for her to tell my Dad about my relationship with Mike, as he had become very suspicious that Mike had turned up at the hospital, but none of my other friends had bothered. I gave her the permission she wanted and looking back, I think that was because I simply didn't care about much at the time. I had really shut my emotions down. My Dad's response was honestly amazing finding out that his son was in a same-sex relationship. He was more angry than I had kept it from him all this time. My eldest brother Adam told me how proud he was of me and I think that was the first proper conversation that we had had since he had found me overdosed with my eyes falling to the back of my head. He hugged me and told me he loved me. We all thought it would be best if Adam was the person who told our other brother Connah. He always seemed to take news better from Adam than anyone else and being completely honest, we all were a little unsure about how he would feel about having a gay brother. His response was iconic and we still laugh about it today. Adam had done his speech about how I'm still their brother and then he told him that Mike and I were together as a couple. Connah's reply, "That's obvious, get out my room and stop making a big deal out of it" and carried on playing on his Xbox and that was it, all my family knew. All because I had done this overdose, the truth had finally come out. I should have been happy about them finding out. Their reaction and support was incredible, but in reality, I didn't like them knowing. I'd enjoyed this secret and private life for over a year now and now it was exposed to other people on the outside. I felt like I had signed a contract that now stated from today and all my future days that I would identify as solely gay, and there would be no going back or get out of jail free card with this one. I now had no idea where my life was going and in 12 months, my life had completely changed and I didn't know how I fitted in with it anymore.

Shortly after "coming out" to my family, I suffered my first bit of discrimination. After the overdose, I wanted to give back to the NHS for saving my life and use my experience to help others. I decided I wanted to become an organ and blood donor. I signed up online to become an organ donor and proudly hold my card in my wallet to this day. However, donating my blood wasn't as easy. I signed up online too and went along to the next clinic they had at a local hotel. Upon arriving, I was given a form to fill in before it took place.

The form just seemed to be simple questions of personal details such as name, age, date of birth and background information. Until it came to two questions that asked about my sexual history—it asked if I had unprotected sex with a female in the past 12 months. The answer to this was yes. Then it asked if I had unprotected sex with a male in the past three months. The answer to this was also yes. I could have lied like I was doing to so many. I could have said I hadn't had sex with the same gender, but I decided to start being honest with others and also with myself and ticked the box that said "yes". After handing the form back in, I was pulled aside and in hearing distance of others waiting and told that they could not accept my blood donation as I had had sex with a male in the past 12 months. I felt humiliated. As I embarrassingly left the hotel, I had so many questions running through my head, why would they not accept my blood as it is tested anyway? Why would they accept my blood if I'd had sex with a female, but not with a male? Wouldn't they test that anyway? If Sarah came to donate blood and she'd had sex with me, who'd had sex with a male, surely her blood would be tested too? Of course, I understood this was due to the likelihood of having HIV, but I felt it was wrong to assume that Sarah or any other blood would be clear and assume that mine wouldn't. I left the clinic and I felt completely different to everyone around me. This was a moment I questioned if I could cope with being openly gay. Was I always going to have to declare myself as homosexual for medical procedures? Was I always going to be seen as dirty or infectious? Were people always going to wonder if I had HIV? By this upcoming summer, I'm happy to see that the rules regarding gay men donating blood are becoming relaxed and will see gay men who have been in long-term relationship being able to donate their blood.

My relationship with Mike grew stronger after the second overdose. We became a complete couple without even realising it. Only the weekend after the overdose, he took me away to stay over in a hotel in Blackpool. We walked through Blackpool together, not holding hands or any public display of affection—that's just not us, but together in public instead of hidden away in a car, my bedroom or a hotel room and that was a huge step for us. Eventually, he asked me to start coming to watch his gigs with his band, so I could get to know his band members and his friends who sometimes went watching too but without them knowing we were a couple (although we found out since the majority of them had worked it out quickly). The issue became that his family, friends and everyone apart from my own family had no idea about us. Although that was ok for a while, it became a consistent problem in our relationship and very nearly destroyed it. We did start to branch out a little bit more, going to restaurants and the cinema together, but it would always be trying to avoid people that we may know. We booked our first holiday together to Portugal that year. It felt very alien to be in a foreign country together where nobody knew us, eating meals and drinking drinks together and not having to wonder if someone we knew was going to walk in. Although this holiday was a great experience, it was definitely a learning curve for Mike. Mike had never really been in a relationship before ours, so holidays to him were usually "lads holidays" and a few times on this holiday, he needed reminding that he didn't need to do push-ups in the apartment before going down to the pool. He didn't need to impress anyone and didn't need to make eye contact with girls in the nightclubs or be made up when he noticed them looking over at him because he wouldn't be bringing them back to our apartment. After we had a conversation over it, I realised this was all new to him and it was that little bit more difficult to adjust to because I was male. But in all, those four days in Portugal really did put our love for each other to the test and fortunately, we passed with success (For those still wondering, I had told Mike by this point that I loved him back - it was in my bedroom as he held me, the smile on his face as I said the words he'd been waiting to hear, I'll never forget that). We had a funny experience in Portugal. When we arrived, the hotel receptionist was confused by two males sharing a room together and apologised that the hotel room they were providing us was a king-size bed only, we assured her it was perfectly fine, but she insisted that they would have the bed changed to separate the following day. The next day, she came to find us around the pool and again apologised for the bed situation until we repeatedly told her we were ok with sharing a bed. None of us felt comfortable in saying we wanted the bed to be together as we were a couple.

It's sad but true, but the day after getting home from the hospital I insisted on returning to work straight away. I had taken the overdose on Sunday, been released from hospital on Monday evening and then returned to work Tuesday. The main reason for my insistence to return to work as I didn't want my new bosses to find out about my demons and view me as unreliable. I had only just started to work for this young couple in December, and I couldn't begin to imagine how they would feel if two months later that the boy they had hired to run their new barbershop was completely unstable and unreliable that he had quite nearly never turned up for work on the Tuesday due to, well, death. The conditions of returning were that I had to be dropped off there and picked back up by either my parents, brothers or siblings and they would be continuously calling and texting throughout the day to check up on me. Nobody could blame them, they were absolutely terrified, but I still didn't care how it was affecting them. I just didn't want to be here anymore and was simply just going through the motions of a day pretending to be alive and present. One safety net I had was my work life. I always felt more confident in myself when I was working. People would praise my work and become returning customers coming back to me, some even asking for me instead of the other barbers/hairdressers that I worked with and that always felt amazing, and I'm so grateful for my customers and still am to this day. The first salon that I worked in, I had walked in as a shy boy, training as an apprentice and who rarely said more than two sentences to the customers. Throughout the years, I developed the confidence to make and initiate the conversation with strangers and had returning clientele. In my first workplace, the salon had been such a great laugh to work in, I made a friend for life in Laura there and we continue to be best friends today and now work in another salon together. Other friends who I was incredibly close to and my mentor who had built me up with the practical and business knowledge to eventually become a successful barber. However, one woman worked there and she did everything she could to make my life hell. I definitely built my good work ethic because there was no slacking around her, even if she would be sitting on her phone whilst she made all these demands. She was the manager of the shop, in all honesty, a complete nasty piece of work. She seemed to thrive on bullying the younger staff and on the first day in the salon with her, she told me, "We probably won't like each other but let's just get along for the sake of work, ok?" I just timidly responded with "Ok". I was so scared of her that I was once hit by a car running for the bus on my way to work. After being thrown onto the bonnet of the car and slapping back down on the road, I continued to run for the bus out of pure fear that she would shout at me for being late for work. Fortunately, I did get there on time, even before her, but I arrived with incredibly bruised ribs that she claimed, "look fine, you'll survive the day".

Luckily I did without any lasting damage. After a year of this woman making me dread work every single day, making me clean the skirting boards with a toothbrush, forcing me to clean the industrial bin outside, weed the garden, even my own wage packet that had been placed above the ceiling tile and stand upstairs one day because she "couldn't be arsed" with me that day, she finally left after having a baby and I truly believe that was when I started to develop my confidence into becoming the barber I am today. So I thank her for the life lessons that she taught me. I have learnt a great work ethic and most importantly, how not to treat people just because you can put a manager as your job status on Facebook. Unfortunately, my best friend Laura also left to start her maternity leave and the shop was no longer the same experience for me. The original owner, who had been my mentor, sold the shop to an accountant who did nothing but allowed the business to run to the ground, so eventually, I jumped the sinking ship. I left the salon in December after I was poached by the couple who wanted me to run their shop for them. The following month, the original salon I had worked in ceased trading.

Although it was a good step to make, I don't think the new salon's environment helped my mental health. I was completely secluded with no other members of staff. The salon was brand new and seriously struggling to build a new clientele up. It was lucky if it had more than ten people come in a day most days, usually having around 4 or 5 customers. With way too much time to think, all I did was overthink and two months later, I had made that second suicide attempt in the previous chapter. After only five months of working, the owners refused to pay me any holiday pay and thought "because the shop isn't busy enough" was a justifiable reason to do this. After some investigating, I found out that they had been deducting tax and national insurance from my wage but not paying it to the HMRC, so I was left with no choice but to leave with immediate effect. I went solo and worked as a freelance mobile barber for a short while and continued building my confidence in my own work and myself as a person each day.

I was approached during my time as a mobile barber by two barbershops to come work for them. Both these positions were full time and offered very similar wages, I originally had refused one of them, but they messaged again asking if I was sure, so we arranged a trial day. Both trial days at each salon were successful and I was grateful that both seemed very interested in having me work for them. It was a massive confidence booster for someone who had always struggled to make his way into groups of friends, so the fact that these two salons wanted me to work for them was such an amazing feeling. I went with the salon that I had originally declined; I had no idea as to why other than it was closer to home and I actually enjoyed the trial at the other shop a little bit more. It is not a decision that I regretted. At this salon, I got to meet some amazing customers who are still my customers today, some have become more like friends and I slowly admitted that I was gay if people would ask if I was single or if I had a girlfriend. The more strangers I told, the more I accepted it and felt myself embracing my true self instead of suppressing my thoughts and feelings. Although I no longer work at this salon today, I didn't really enjoy my employment there and it unfortunately, didn't end on the best of terms, I am so grateful for those two years of my life because that was when I became "Josh The Barber" and a lot of my personal life changed for the better during my time there. I went into this barbershop in the closet, shy and recovering from depression with a recent suicide attempt, to becoming a friendly, happy lad in a long-term same-sex relationship and slowly reducing my medication dosage.

I decided halfway through that year to tell my friend James that I was gay. After previously not having a good response from my former friends, it was a nerve-wracking situation to finally tell one of my other best friends. We were out celebrating his birthday with his family when I asked him for a chat. Then I told him everything, all about myself, about my relationship with Mike and my previous situation with Charlie. Luckily, he believed me and he stood by me, accepting me for exactly who I was. Once I told him everything, he said that it made much more sense and he believed I was telling the truth. Charlie had been telling people lies about me, telling them that I had attempted to make a move on him, and when he rejected me, that was when we fell out. He was trying to destroy any credibility that I had, and of course, with me being a medicated unstable depressive, it made it an easy story to believe. It was so frustrating and the people he had lied to that after a few weeks I acted on anger and regret my action now, but I felt that if he was going to publicly out me before I was ready, why should I give him any respect. I spoke to his girlfriend, Jodie and I sent her some screenshots of the text between him and me around the time of our secret affair. Unfortunately, she chose not to believe me and blocked my number. I can only suspect that she was either manipulated into believing that I had made it all up, or secretly she knew the truth but didn't want to believe it. But I didn't try it to expose the truth any further. I accepted some people wouldn't believe me, most probably didn't, but the people closest to me knew and those around the time who couldn't be manipulated or blinded by lies did too. That was my past and I was no longer spending my time worrying about it. If the real Charlie or the real Jodie are reading this now, I wish you both every bit of happiness. You both deserve happiness too.

Throughout the year, Mike and I had had many discussions over our potential but unsure future. While in the car at our usual old spot, one discussion had Mike telling me he wasn't sure what he wanted for the future and wasn't sure if he ever wanted to tell people. I respected his honesty but told him that it now meant that we could no longer be together much longer then, I couldn't live the rest of my life as a dirty secret. I think the idea of not having me around made him realise how much he wanted to keep having me in his life. The day we went back to his house, his parents were away on holiday, but he left it up to fate if I met his sister Natalie. Of course, that day I got to meet Natalie, don't forget I had already been kicked out of a nightclub by her as Sarah's friend, but they were no longer close friends so now I was meeting her as Mike's sister. I think she knew straight away what was going on. She arrived with her boyfriend Kieran, who I had been to school with. I was worried that because I was continuously called "faggot" and "queer" in school (never by Kieran), it wouldn't take them long to figure out what was going on anyway, even if we did sit miles apart from one another watching Game of Thrones. After they left, Mike must have been really stressed out, but I think he also felt relieved too. He didn't want to sit down and have a conversation with people about it, so it was easier to let them assume, which was ok for me.

On Valentine's Day, our last together that we couldn't publicly celebrate, we sat in my bedroom at home and watched films together when Mike received a Snapchat from a work colleague, a female work colleague, a name I'd noted coming up throughout the previous months. I'll openly admit I had zero trust and was extremely paranoid and expected Mike was too good to be true, so I over-thought situations and became very sensitive to them. I noticed he hadn't opened the notification until he asked me to go downstairs to make him a cup of tea. I knew what was going on—I had been that person trying to hide things. When I got back to the bedroom, I clicked on his phone, and the notification was gone. I quizzed him on what the message was, and he made some awful attempt at lying that it was just a general one that had also been put on her public story. You'd think that would be enough for an explanation, wouldn't you? But not for me at the time. Minutes later, I asked to see the story, he showed me her public story, but it was 7 hours old, not 20 minutes old, when the notification had come through. I knew he was lying to me and he knew I knew too, but he tried his best to get out of it. After giving him the choices of telling the truth or leaving for good, he finally admitted that he had lied to protect my feelings as she had sent something I wouldn't seem as appropriate and wouldn't like to be sent to him. I won't go into what it was, as she has apologised to me through Mike, and she had no idea that he was in a relationship or gay, so she was innocent. By this time, I was beyond fed up with the secret and it felt like nothing was going to change any time soon, but he promised he would tell this work colleague the following day so it wouldn't happen again. He stuck to his promise and slowly, Mike began to open up to people and himself.

One night, Mike was rehearsing with his band. I was at home in my bedroom when I got a text from him to say "I've told my Mum". I originally had no idea what he was talking about, but then the following text explained: "about you". I wish he had done it differently—knowing his Mum Catherine—she deserves a lot better than a text, but mid-rehearsing, he decided now was the time and sent her a pre-written text explaining about our relationship. She was absolutely amazed by the news and insisted I come around to visit her as soon as possible. When I finally got to meet her, she hugged me and could see how nervous I was. She softly said, "it's so amazing you can both be together, be happy and be who you want to be in society today". Adding in true Catherine style said, "Keep fighting for the fight". If there is ever a perfect mother-in-law, it is Catherine.

She is so gentle, spiritual and such a kind person. Although we have never sat down and had a conversation about my past experiences, I feel like she completely understands what I've been through and how it affects me every single day. Their dog, Max, gave away that he'd known me for a little while as when I walked in, Catherine warned me, "Max can be wary of strangers". The next minute he was jumping up on my knee, drowning me in kisses. I wasn't a stranger to Max.

Mike's sister Natalie was also amazing at introducing me into the family. She immediately planned an outing together with her boyfriend Kieran. The four of us went for an Italian tapas and bowling. She seemed to enjoy getting to know me, and I think she was mesmerised by how my mind works. Natalie is a really clever girl and quickly picked up on that I had been through some stuff and now she is one of the people I really do open up to. We don't always agree on everything, we have discussions where the two of us have completely different viewpoints and I love that. She is very straight to the point and will say exactly how she feels—the complete opposite to how I am, so I find her mesmerising and completely terrifying at the same time. Natalie is very passionate about her family and when she became very protective over me too, I knew then that she saw me as her family. She does get very angry when people have hurt me, I'm sure she has been very angry whilst reading this book . She does also get angry with me about my small appetite and once told me that I had to go into training to eat bigger portions of food before I was allowed to become a true Gaskell. Although there are times when Natalie is a lot to handle, I'm forever grateful that she is my sister-in-law. She truly did and still makes me feel like a family member and not just because I am in a relationship with her brother.

Mike's Dad, Ian, struggled with the news that his son was gay at first and needed some time to get his head around it before he was ready to meet me. At the time, I was really hurt, angry, frustrated, but mostly devastated that someone had rejected me and took it far too personal, but now I understand that wasn't the case at all. Ian is a very private man and it was a lot to take in and adjust to, but once he was ready, I was invited around to meet him and have a night all together as a family, and I've been welcomed in their home ever since. I do actually think out of us all, his kids and their partners, I am his favourite. I feel like I understand Ian a lot where others don't seem to, and he understands and respects when I'm not comfortable with something—usually it is trying new things or Natalie attempting to get me drunk.

I absolutely loved meeting Mike's Gran, Pat, she is such a warm-hearted lady. She immediately took me under her wing and accepted me into her family. We have some amazing conversations, and I love hearing stories of when she was younger and her relationship with Alan, Mike's Grandad. Pat reminds me of my own Nan and how accepting she would have been of Mike. Every time we go see Pat, she has a way of making you feel so loved and appreciated that it makes me hate leaving. It usually takes Mike to remind me we have plans or need to do something that we leave. I remember when she introduced me to Mike's Grandad, Alan. He was lying in his bed in the living room due to a stroke he had 17 years previously and struggling with dementia; I don't think he knew who or what I was, but he acknowledged I was there. The following year at Christmas, I looked over at Alan sitting in his wheelchair and he gave me a smile with his eyes and said, "You alright?" This was a common phrase from him that I had saw him say to his children and grandchildren, so when I was asked the question I truly felt on cloud nine, Alan must have recognised me as family now. We sadly lost Alan only two years after I met him. He passed away just before Christmas leaving a massive hole in all his family's hearts. I got to know more about Alan and his life after his passing than I did when he was here with us and I wish I could go back and get to know more about him from himself.. I am proud to say I now have this man's surname as my own and I hope I can make him proud.

I first met Mike's Grandad Colin, his Mum's Dad, on Boxing Day and I stupidly got his name wrong and called him by his surname Owen. I went bright red in the face and couldn't sit down quick enough. I was so nervous about meeting this man and was fuming with myself for getting off to a bad start. He made a joke about my ripped jeans and my tattoos and he still does to this day, but he seemed to like me and liked that I was a barber. Colin is a very emotional man and I love that even with his generation being very private about emotions, he isn't afraid to show his . It's so obvious with Colin that his children and grandchildren mean the world to him and it's a privilege to be classed as family.

I enjoy being part of Mike's family, especially during the Christmas season, as traditionally, they all meet up and share presents. I remember the first Christmas after Mike came out, I went to his Gran's with him and was in shock when his aunties, uncles and cousins had also bought me presents. I didn't even expect to receive anything from anyone. They all truly have gone out of their way to make me feel like family, and I do. I see them as my family now, and I thoroughly enjoy it when there are family get-togethers at either Grandparent's house. It's something I miss terribly with my own family.

It was one thing Mike telling his family about us but telling his friends was another story. My former group of friends hadn't reacted so well to the news and although many of my other friends, including James, Olivia and Gabrielle, had been amazing, I was still petrified that Mike was going to lose people. Mike is very sporty. He enjoys playing cricket and golf. It's commonly known that a cricketer will always put cricket first above anything else. I was worried that he would feel that uncomfortable after telling his friends that he would have to leave it behind, especially if they didn't accept him. I didn't want to be the reason he lost people the way I did. Mike decided he didn't want to have a serious conversation with each one of his friends, so the only other way to let everyone know without having that conversation was through social media—putting it on Facebook. Mike's friend's reactions surprised us both. Mike returned home and hid under his duvet as the messages of support poured through, every single one of his friends reached out in happiness for him. It really was a beautiful thing to watch the stress and anxiety leave him as he realised his friends still loved him no matter who he was in a relationship with. Months previous to going public with Mike, I texted Sarah asking her for a conversation, it felt only right that she should know before I told my friends and I was incredibly nervous to tell her. She accepted the chance to talk together so we drove to Starbucks and talked over a hot chocolate. I confessed everything to her.

I couldn't tell her Mike's name, only that I was in a relationship with a male and about my brief affair with Charlie. She was very supportive and we continued to stay in touch with one another for months afterwards. She was suffering from her own insecurities and mental health issues at the time, and I felt like we confided in one another in our recoveries. The night Mike and I went public on Facebook, I texted her to let her know of our plans, she repeated how proud she was of us. Unfortunately, once the Facebook relationship changed to 'in a relationship' together, she blocked all contact with me. I have been told since that she told many that I never had the decency to tell her about Mike, which was hurtful as I believed I did everything I could to put her feelings first when it came to the matter of going public with my relationship with Mike. We haven't spoken since. I respect her wishes and have never tried to contact her. I am told that she is doing really well for herself and I'm proud of the accomplishments she has achieved since our time together. If the real Sarah is reading this, thank you for helping me grow, thank you for teaching me how to be loved and to love and I'm sorry for all the pain we put each other through. You deserve every bit of happiness there is.

The world finally knew about my and Mike's relationship. Every single one of Mike's friends had welcomed me with open arms and made an effort to get to know me. These were true friends, friends who accepted him for exactly who they knew he was and not what he hoped they thought he would be. That year was going from strength to strength. I was in such a brilliant place mentally that I decided to sit down with my doctor and put in a request that I start to make reductions in my medication. It would be a lengthy and complex process due to the high dosage that I had to take. I felt like if there was any time to start reducing them, it was when my life seemed positive and stronger than ever before.

CHAPTER TEN

Everything seemed to be going really well. For the first time in 4 years, I no longer had to hide who I was. Our relationship was completely public knowledge and the love and support we received had been amazing. After we changed our relationship status on Facebook to "in a relationship" with one another, we received over 300 likes and lots of comments. I noticed whenever I uploaded a photo of us together, it always seemed to get a lot of love and support. I once said to Mike, "Facebook loves the gays". At this point, the word "gay" was still very alien to us, and Mike was struggling with identifying himself as gay but was comfortable with everyone else knowing of our relationship. He had taken huge steps; I couldn't have been more proud of him. I was taking steps myself. I was frequently going to the gym and starting to appreciate myself as a person. I had managed to reduce from 45mg of Mirtazapine down to 30mg and was in discussions and preparations with my doctor to further reduce in the upcoming months. This year was going from strength to strength, not only for our relationship but for my family. We had just found out that my eldest brother Adam and his fiancee Rachael were expecting their first child together. This would be my parent's first grandchild, my first niece/nephew, and Adam was the first in the family tree to have his own offspring coming into the world, so everybody was more than excited. The pregnancy came to mean more to us, as a few short weeks after finding out my Rachael was pregnant, she started to bleed and we all were really worried that the baby we had all got so excited to meet may not be coming to join us after all. Fortunately, after attending a private scan as there was very little help from the NHS advisors, we were thrilled to find out that their little baby still had a strong heartbeat and everything was going perfectly fine with the pregnancy.

This year, I was turning 22, the number had always been unlucky for me, so I really wasn't looking forward to turning this age. I'd never really looked forward to my birthdays. My 21st didn't have the best of builds up due to a conflict with a family member regarding Mike keeping our relationship a secret, which resulted in Mike not being able to come to the birthday celebration meal. My 20th birthday had been the start of the most toxic relationship in my life, so I'd lost the excitement for birthdays a while back. However, I was looking forward to 22nd May, this was planned to be a much more exciting day than a stupid birthday as it was the day I was finally getting to see the incredible performer Ariana Grande. I'd become a massive fan of her in the past few years and ever since the awful year that I had had in 2015, I became really attached to her and related to her lyrics. I successfully managed to purchase two overpriced tickets being resold rather late on and could not wait to finally see her and hear her vocals live. I was going with my Gabrielle. We had always been really close since college but had become incredibly close in the previous 12 months and most of our time together. She was my rock, my best friend.

My parents went away on holiday the night before the concert, my eldest brother Adam had moved into his own house with Rachael the previous year and my other brother Connah had gone back to spend a third season in Ibiza. I rushed out of the house as quickly as I could, getting excited as I collected Gabrielle and we were on our way to Manchester, playing an Ariana Grande playlist loudly and chatting away to each other. As we got about halfway there, Gabby innocently asked me, "Have you got the tickets, yeah?" My heart stopped. I checked every pocket and place in the car, but I knew I had stupidly left the tickets at home as I was rushing out. Idiot! I was such an idiot! I did a u-turn as soon as I could and sped all the way back home—I won't openly admit to the speed I was doing, but I was rushing to get home as we were risking missing the opening of the show. Stress levels went incredibly high. Gabby was really supportive and although I could tell she was stressed too, she did her best to laugh it off and tried to keep me calm. Finally, when I got home, I rushed into the house, grabbed the tickets and off we went again. When we finally arrived at the arena, the surrounding area was so quiet, and it made me panic that there were no queues. Had the show started already? Surely we weren't the only ones who hadn't made it in time to watch the opening acts. We pulled into a car parking space across the arena and rushed along the street to get to the show. Rushing into the arena with excitement and stress, we had no idea what we were about to experience.

As we were allocated our seats at the back row on the floor seats, something didn't seem quite right. I tried to explain to a staff member that the tickets I purchased weren't on the floor. We were meant to be on the first row of the first tier. When I purchased them, I was relieved that nobody would be directly in front of us and blocking our view. But the staff member insisted these were our seats, and there must have been a change in the layout. I wasn't impressed as the view was strained with many many people standing directly in front of us. All different heights and some even had their children placed on their shoulders, blocking our view even more. We had only just made it in time for the show countdown to come on the screen, Ariana smiling away, encouraging the crowd on a pre-recorded video on the screens that displayed the countdown. I couldn't believe we had made it. The arena being so hot, Gabby complained about the heat and I could feel my t-shirt sticking to my back underneath the open shirt I had on. The show was incredible and it felt completely surreal to know we were in the same room as Ariana Grande, although the view was very strained. We tried to move into the aisle to watch, as a father with his child on his shoulders repeatedly blocked our view, but a staff member told us that we had to return to our seats for health and safety reasons as it was dangerous to block the aisles. I remember rolling my eyes. It seemed like they were pathetic, not allowing us to just stand there so we could see and ridiculous to call it dangerous. However, there was something far more dangerous happening.

The concert ended and we made our way to the steps on the tiers that would lead us out of the arena into the foyer. However, staff members blocked this stairway for those whose seats were on the floor, and we were told to go to the stairs that went underneath the arena located at either side of the arena. During our time in this stairway, Salman Ramadan Abedi, a 22-year-old the same age as me, detonated a bomb packed with nuts and bolts in the foyer, killing 22 innocent people and injuring hundreds more. I remember hearing a rumble and an uproar of screaming, but I never suspected anything dangerous had just happened just above us. I turned to Gabby and said, "I hope she's not come back on stage", believing the uproar of screaming could be due to the excitement of the crowd and not fear and pain. The sound of those screams is something that still troubles me to this day. I remember being pushed from behind, feeling the pressure on my back and my feet leaving the ground at one point and then all of sudden, we had gone through some doors that led us straight outside. The atmosphere was confusing and alarming and we had no idea what had just happened. Everywhere you looked, people were running and it became evident immediately something wasn't quite right. As we stood on the side of the pavement, a man ran into me, almost knocking the wind out of me and I feared that I would fall onto the merchandise stall on the floor. I turned to this stranger in anger and heard the words "Run" and then had continued running and was gone. Gabby and I constantly just looked at one another in confusion and started to make our way back to the car park. Everyone was running. Nobody was walking at a normal pace. There was a feeling of complete and utter panic in the air. We must have looked like a deer in headlights and a very emotional and frantic girl close to us came over to explain. "A bomb's just gone off," she said, looking around in panic. Her face looked like she had been crying. "A bomb? Where?" I asked, but she said she didn't know and was pulled away by her friend. She left us with that information and then was gone. I am ashamed to admit that I didn't believe her at the time and if that girl is somehow reading this, I'm so sorry I wasn't any comfort to you that night, and I thank you for taking your time to try and help us in that horrible situation. As we walked, I saw a woman crying at the side, she was saying she had heard a massive bang and then saw a young girl being carried out with a lot of blood on her. I turned to Gabby and asked, "What should we do?", she looked in complete distress and her instant reply was, "Can we just go home now?" so we made our way quickly back to the car. I paid for the car parking machine with my token, which felt strange that we still had to pay with what was happening, then finally we got to the car. I tried ringing Mike several times, Gabby was ringing people on her own phone too, but we couldn't get a signal. Eventually, I got through to Mike. I explained what we had been told had happened after the concert and he checked social media and the news and confusingly told us there was nothing reported. We sat in an extremely large queue of cars trying to leave the car park all at the same time, so I scrolled through Twitter and came across a post that said a speaker had blown at the end of the concert. I instantly began to settle down and explained to my Gabby that people must be assuming it was a bomb, but it really was just the speaker blowing. But that didn't explain the woman who had said she had seen a young girl with a lot of blood. Maybe she had put 2 and 2 together and got 5 instead of 4? But she hadn't. She had got the right answer. Mike went quiet on the phone after making a small noise of shock. We both asked him, "What?" And "What's wrong?" He then asked me where we were in relation to the arena, so I explained again that we were stuck in the car park opposite trying to get off. He then calmly explained that Sky News had reported that a bomb had gone off inside the arena and it was a terrorist attack. I instantly felt sick. As the news confirmed what had happened, a very loud siren began to play from somewhere, saying, "This is an emergency, please evacuate the area" repeatedly, over and over again. After hearing this sound on repeat for 45–60 minutes, it still to this day haunts me.

At no point in life can you ever expect to be anywhere near something as horrendous as a terrorist attack. I was not mentally prepared for this experience. Neither of us was. I just wanted to get home, and I wanted to be at home where it was safe. Gabby broke the silence when she innocently asked if cars are bulletproof. Unfortunately, my little red Vauxhall Corsa was not and we both felt vulnerable sitting there waiting for our turn to get off the car park. The queue for the cars was no longer several lines of cars. It was just an incredibly large semi-circle of cars beeping, bumper to bumper, doing everything they could to get off the car park. I could see the barrier repeatedly going up and down and being in complete disbelief that they weren't allowing everyone in their cars to get off the car park and away from the area as quickly as possible. They continued to check if people had paid for their parking tickets. As we waited, we both began to panic and overthink and eventually, between us we came up with a plan of what we needed to do if another attacker came with a gun. We planned to get to the nearest hotel, a Premier Inn. We said we weren't to wait for one another, and we were to just run as fast as we could to get there. Fortunately, we never had to see this plan through. We just needed to get home.

Once Mike had said the attack was all over the news, the streets were quickly filled with the flashing lights of the emergency services and I knew I needed to contact my brother Adam, it wouldn't be long before he found out what had happened and he needed to know that I was ok. I finally got through to him and told him what we knew at that point and although he seemed really alarmed and worried for me, he was calm and I asked him if he could let our Mum and Dad know as I knew they were going to be really panicked, and I didn't want to reassure them I was fine until I knew that I was completely fine and would only be once I was out of Manchester and back at home. Within minutes of ending the phone call with Adam, my parents were on the phone ringing me. They were obviously extremely worried and needed to know where I was and what was going on. I explained that we were stuck in the car park opposite the arena. My Mum begged me to get out of the car and run to safety, but I knew I wouldn't feel safe until I was back at home, so I insisted on staying in the car and getting Gabby and me home. We needed to get away from here. After a while, the barrier was permanently lifted in the car park. Around an hour later, we were finally on the road driving away from the arena. Away from the emergency sirens and away from the flashing lights of police, ambulances and fire engines. My phone was continuously ringing or notifying me of messages as people were realising that I had attended the concert. I ignored most of the calls as I wanted to feel safe before reassuring people that I was. The streets of Manchester were chaotic. The rules of the road seemed to have gone out the window as people drove through red lights, swerved into lanes and did U-Turns in the middle of busy roads. I remember thinking, "We've been lucky to have survived a bomb attack, but we are going to lose our lives on the roads here." Once we got onto the motorway leaving Manchester, the roads went from chaotic to complete stillness. There weren't any other cars travelling into Manchester. It seemed the motorway had been closed off, the only cars were the ones leaving the city. This scene made Gabby become really emotional as she shouted, "Why are there no cars there?! Why is nobody going there?!"

I finally got her home and then I realised that my car desperately needed petrol. I had been running low the whole journey home and hadn't even realised.

I must have been running on adrenaline because as I went to a petrol station around the corner, my hands were trembling so much that I couldn't get the petrol nozzle into the car. The staff member working inside the petrol station spoke over a microphone to explain I needed to put the nozzle into the car before he sensed something wasn't right. He came outside asking if I was ok and as I looked up at him, he looked startled, he asked what was wrong and I explained that I had just been at a concert in Manchester. I was shocked that he knew exactly what had happened and instantly got me to sit down next to the car, he filled my car up with petrol for me and went inside and brought me a hot chocolate from the instant machine. He asked me to drink the hot chocolate and calm myself down before getting back into my car to drive. I never got to thank him, so if that man is reading this, thank you so much for helping me in that situation. It really was much appreciated. I think I was just too much in shock to show this.

Adam rang me just after I left the petrol station and asked if I had made it home yet, I explained I had dropped Gabby off at her home and was on my way back home. He told me to ring him back once I got home and I knew that he knew something more and wanted me to be not driving when he told me. I repeatedly asked what it was, what he knew and he eventually admitted that it had been confirmed on the news that people had died due to the explosion in the arena. My heart just stopped. I don't remember any of the drive home after that point; I don't even remember how the rest of the conversation went. I just remember feeling in complete and utter shock. When I finally arrived home, I pulled onto the drive, and my front door was open slightly. Had I left it like that? Had someone broken in? This surely couldn't be happening after what I just experienced. I slowly went into the house, listening out for any movements, going to the kitchen first, turning every light on as I went through and I grabbed a knife out of the rack for protection just in case someone had broken in. I went into the living room and our dog Oscar (the son of our original dog Jasper and my Nan's dog Megan) was lying down on the sofa in complete peace. I was pretty sure then that I must have been so stressed out when I forgot the tickets that I didn't realise I hadn't shut or locked the door, but I still investigated the rest of the house. My phone started to ring again. It was my friend Olivia. She rang to check that I was ok and sounded so relieved to hear my voice. I reassured her that I was fine but still slightly in shock. Gabby phoned too to tell me that her boyfriend had collected her from her house and was taking her home with him as he didn't want her to spend the night on her own. I remember feeling jealous that Mike hadn't done the same for me. Maybe he was in shock too and wasn't sure how to react, but it is something that irritated me for a little while that he didn't get his stuff and come stay at my house with me. He did text and ring to make sure I was at home in bed and I went to sleep, hoping the feeling of shock would wear off by the morning.

 The feeling of shock did wear off, but it was only replaced by the feeling of stress, anxiety and guilt. Around 3.30 am, my FitBit watch recorded that I had shot up awake from my sleep and my heart rate rose drastically high. I think that was the moment the adrenaline wore off and my brain started to digest what it had just witnessed. I sat for around an hour or so crying to myself and feeling a huge amount of guilt. I watched the headlines coming in and read every article there was, watching news presenters break the news to the rest of the world, the death figure rising and the sadness of the country setting in. I noticed I kept hearing the number 22, my unlucky number. I turned 22 two days before 22nd May and another 22-year-old came and disgustingly murdered 22 people. My head told me it was my fault and that I was a bad omen for everyone. These people died because I went there. Was forgetting the tickets meant to be a sign? Was this punishment for all the things I'd done? Was this a punishment for attempting to take my own life several times? How could I still be alive when these people had died? Surely they deserved to live more than I did. I must have fallen back asleep at some point because my alarm for work woke me the next day. Work. How on earth was I going to go to work that day? How was I going to stand and cut peoples hair whilst they talked and gossiped about the events of the night before, the event I was at and wasn't ready to register, never mind talk about. My Mum rang me in the morning to tell me she was booking a flight home, but I made her promise to stay on her holiday, they needed this holiday and I didn't want to be the reason they came home early. I was planning on going to work, so it meant they would only be coming home from their holiday and spend the day waiting for me to get home from work, it seemed pointless, so I begged them to stay. But I did really want them to come home. I can openly admit at that moment I needed my Mum to hug me, hold me and tell me I was safe, but I wasn't the reason their holiday was ruined. I got ready for work, put my uniform on, packed my bag and then I went to leave, but as I went to open the front door, I had a thought in my head that I could have nearly not have returned home yesterday, some people who I had shared a room with hadn't made it home and my brain convinced me at that moment that if I left the house that day that I wouldn't return. I locked the door and phoned one of the members of the family who owned the salon. I explained that I had been at the concert the night before and I didn't feel like I could work that day, her reply was she would speak to the owner, her relative and see what he said about it. I felt a little taken back at that moment as I wasn't asking permission to have the day off. I was telling them I couldn't work. I wasn't contracted at their business; I was paid cash in hand, so if I didn't feel fit enough to work, I had no obligation to go into work that day and I was being made to wait to see if I was given permission for the day off. She rang back and told me, of course I could have the day off and expressed her concern for me and was really lovely about how I must be feeling. The boss rang not long after, but he wasn't as understanding as his relative. He laughed that I had no need to feel anxious coming into work as "ISIS aren't going to blow up the shop mate", a statement that may have been true but was completely insensitive. I expressed I wasn't ready to talk about the night before and customers would be talking about it. He told me to "Tell them you don't want to talk about it then", he had zero understanding of how I was feeling, so I just repeated that I wouldn't be working that day, so he accepted that and told me, "Have the day off so you can get your head sorted for tomorrow". My colleague rang to tell me they had asked her to cover my shift, but she refused as she thought it would be insensitive and she also told me that the family who owned the business were annoyed with me for not working that day.

    I spent the morning watching and reading more articles as the names of the victims started to be reported. I remember there being an appeal to find a girl named Olivia. I hoped and hoped that she had just gotten lost in the crowds. I didn't want her to be one of the victims; I even saw a Facebook post saying she had been found. However, it wasn't true and sadly she was announced as one of the victims. She was 15-years-old, the age I had been when I first planned to attempt to end my life. Why her? Why was she taken from her family when she had her full life ahead of her and I got to sit there after several attempts of ending my life, completely fine. The next victim who stood out for me was little

Saffie. This broke me. I cried and cried over Saffie being one of the victims. How had I survived this over an 8-year-old-girl? What right did I have to survive that and she did not? Why was she taken from her family, and I sat there completely unharmed?

Gabby was also struggling that day, so she came to the house for the day and we grieved together. We sat and watched the news together all day, we read articles, read people's comments on social media and discussed how we were feeling. We were an incredible support system for one another at the time and it's something nobody else will understand unless they were there that night. In the evening my boss from work rang me again and told me that they needed me to work the following day rather than the shop being closed for another day. I admitted defeat and I agreed to work rather than having the tension of conflict. I didn't want to, nor did I feel ready to, but I didn't have it in me to argue back with him. I can say now that going into work really did help. I remember a girl who I now class as a good friend came in with her young boy for his haircut and was incomplete and utter shock that I was at work. I explained the phone calls from the boss and was absolutely disgusted and demanded to speak to the family. Two of the family members worked in the back of the shop running another business, but they had taken that day off to go shopping in Liverpool—another thing that felt a little disappointing, it was appropriate for them to take a day off to go shopping in Liverpool but not ok for the boy who had been a terrorist attack to take a few days away from work. The topic of the conversation all day was the Manchester concert, and each customer watched as my eyes filled with tears when I explained I had been there and wasn't ready to talk about it just yet. The customers were amazing and so supportive. Many of them are still customers today. I remember that day the radio repeatedly played Ariana Grande's song "One Last Time" and I had to keep muting it until it had finished playing, a song that is still difficult to listen to today.

My parents finally returned home from their holiday that weekend and I couldn't hold back the tears as my Mum, and I just held each other, both of us crying a lot. This is exactly what I had needed, I just needed my Mum and now she was here, I could finally stop being brave and I let everything come out. I cried, explaining the guilt I felt, guilt I still feel. I walked away from that experience with no haunting images, no injuries, no pain of losing a loved one and my life and those 22 people, the hundreds injured and the many who felt the pain of losing family and friends, why did I get to walk away? My parents assured me it just wasn't my time, but it didn't feel like a good enough excuse. I felt like I owed it to those suffering more than I was to make a difference. Each week as I was paid from work, I put aside the amount I needed for outgoings, donating the rest to any of the fundraisers linked to the victims of Manchester. I will openly admit that I became obsessed with what had happened, I spent every free moment googling and looking for more information. I felt like I needed to get to know those who had lost their lives, we had all stood under the same roof, sang the same songs and felt the high atmosphere and I needed to know them. I even messaged poor Olivia's Mum after finding her on social media and expressed my sorrow for her pain and offered any help I could provide to their family.

Two weeks after the concert, I attended the One Love Manchester concert. Originally Gabby was going to come with me, we planned to wear t-shirts she designed for it, but she bravely admitted an hour before we were due to leave, she just couldn't do it. The previous weekend there had been another terrorist attack in London. I had found out about this attack during one of Mike's gigs and instantly asked my parents if we could leave and return home. I just didn't feel safe not being in the family home and all I wanted was to feel safe again. The One Love Manchester concert was an amazing healing experience. It was a rollercoaster of emotions, from bouncing around and dancing in the crowd to sobbing publicly. We originally were seated in a stand far back, but Mike's sister, Natalie, was working at the event and managed to get us a wristband each into the standing section in front of the stage. I was standing next to some of the Parrs Wood High School Choir members who had just sung 'My Everything' with Ariana Grande herself—another song that hits differently ever since the event. I got to meet Imogen Heap. She came out and watched the concert in the golden circle, she hugged me and told me how brave I was to come back to a concert again and hoped I was enjoying the show. Few people knew of Imogen Heap, but I had heard of her work and knew that Ariana Grande was a big fan too, so I was really happy to meet her. Where I was standing, I could see the side of the stage and could see Mac Miller and Miley Cyrus were constantly supporting Ariana. Every time she came off the stage, she would hug either one of them and would have a break from composing her emotions. It was absolutely heartbreaking to watch. At the concert, I decided that I wanted to spend the next year going to as many concerts as I could. I wouldn't let the disgusting act ruin moments like this or stop me from going again. Leaving the concert that day was the hardest part. I was physically shaking as I held Mike's hand so tightly I could feel his pulse, walking past the armed police officers in the street, watching individuals thanking them for making them feel safe. I didn't feel safe. I felt exposed. I have ever since it happened. I've been to many concerts since, including Paloma Faith, Harry Styles, Justin Timberlake, Little Mix and Britney Spears and I've never felt the same leaving a concert since Manchester. I've noticed I constantly have to google the setlist planned for the night, find out what the show's last song will be, and enjoy the concert up until that point. Once that song starts to play, I instantly start to become panicked and begin to shake. The worst feeling was going into the Paloma Faith concert. This was my first concert since the event. Although it was a different arena in a different city, the lack of security was absolutely appalling. After being very briefly hand searched and when I say briefly, I mean hardly even touched me, I started to voice, "I could have a bomb under here and they've not even checked me". Mike rushed me along before I got too angry and the security could hear me. I started to overthink and stress that if I could walk in with an oversized hoodie and a large coat on then, the same thing could happen all over again.

 The first time I went back to the Manchester Arena was to watch Harry Styles. I had bought the tickets for Mike. He will admit that Harry Styles is his guilty pleasure. When Harry performed a song recorded by Ariana and wrote by himself, "Just A Little Bit of Your Heart", I allowed the tears to come out and watched as people raised signs with the One Love Manchester logo on and it really was a special moment. I had the One Love Manchester logo tattooed on my left forearm a month after the attack, adding the Manchester bee on my right middle finger and the same bee Ariana has behind my left ear too. It's something I will always feel connected to and something that has changed my perspective on life. Still to this day, I'm not afraid to admit the event has caused some issues for me. I'm terrified of crowds. I hate being in cities. I dread large gatherings of people, even when I'm not attending them, I don't think I will ever feel the same about a concert again—especially leaving one, but I also feel connected to those who were there the same night too. I met a girl who had been a victim of the Manchester bombing. We met two years after the concert at Ariana Grande's 'Sweetener World Tour' concert in Sheffield. I noticed two girls walking, one struggling to walk in very high heeled boots. She nearly tripped over and had to grab hold of me to stop herself from falling. She apologised to me and we laughed it off and then she and her friend stood next to my Mum and me for the night. The four of us got talking together and then we both confessed that we had been at the Manchester concert two years before. After she told us her story of her injuries and her experience, I felt guilty even saying that I was struggling but was uninjured and had a completely different experience of that night to this poor girl. I have so much respect for her returning to a concert, to Ariana's concert and I'm so grateful she fell on me that night because hearing her story was special. The four of us all got along really well, my Mum bought their drinks and food, and we followed one another on social media after having a picture together. I've really enjoyed seeing both of these girls grow since I met them that night.

After the Manchester concert happened, my doctor decided now wasn't the right time to be experimenting with my medication to see if I could manage another reduction. Whilst I struggled with the aftermath of the event, I was placed back on the highest dosage of the medication until I felt strong enough again one day to start the process of reducing my medication again.

Some of you may view my experience of the Manchester concert as nothing and believe me, I understand why. Some of you may be reading this who experienced much worse that night than I did, and I can't express how much pain I feel for you if you did. I wasn't physically injured or didn't see any horrifying images that night, but I feel like everyone who had attended that concert has been mentally harmed and affected in different ways, but I can only tell my own experience and the pain it caused myself and Gabby. For anyone reading this who has been affected by Manchester, stay strong and well done for getting up each day and proving the disgusting act wrong, acts of violence won't defeat us, it has only brought us together stronger than before.

CHAPTER ELEVEN

2017 started on a high and it managed to end on a high, too, as during the early hours of Christmas Eve morning, my little niece Evie Chelsey Finch was born and instantly took over all of our hearts. I loved seeing Mike holding her tiny little body and how besotted he was with her (don't worry everyone, I still stand by; I don't want my own children no matter how cute Mike looked holding Evie). We were at Mike's gig at a pub, our families spending time together for the first time. Mike's sister Natalie was doing what she does and getting everyone drunk, James had come along to watch him play, and Gabby had started a relationship with my brother Connah once he got back from Ibiza. As I looked around, I really appreciated the moment of having everyone together. Everyone but my eldest brother Adam and his fiancee Rachael, who had just gone into labour at their home and were on their way to the hospital across the road from the gig. I remember holding Evie for the very first time and the release of love for her reduced me to tears. I sat holding her in the quiet living room as she slept and felt the tears falling from my cheeks and everyone else was crying around me. She is so loved and at that moment, I felt so grateful to meet her when we once believed we might not.

After the extreme lows of 2015 and 2016, the high I felt at the start of 2017 had been destroyed by the Manchester concert. I ended the year feeling lost, disconnected from my emotions and without a purpose in life. I was back on the strongest medication and I felt like I had failed in becoming a "normal" human being. Although the year had been difficult once again and more things had been thrown at me, I began to question what else could I possibly be challenged with and I did feel a strength in me growing. I understood that what I had been through was a lot, a therapist had said to me that many wouldn't have been able to face it and I should be proud that I am here today facing it and dealing with it and I did feel proud. I knew that a time for change was coming and I felt ready to find the next project to throw myself into, and that was my career. After the way my employer had acted after the Manchester concert, I knew that my time as their employee was coming to an end and I began searching for alternative employment. I was offered a job in another barbershop and I very nearly took this job. However, it just didn't feel right and that's because I was ready for change, but I wanted to take full control of my career. I had been part of the barbering industry for five years; I had managed three shops, worked with others, worked on my own and helped three shops build their clientele, and built my own clientele with it. A friend had opened up a salon down the road from where I was working and my best friend Laura who I had worked with previously, was renting an area in there too. My friend, Liam, who owned the salon, gave me a proposition to work for myself and set in my own business renting an area in his shop. At the time, I didn't feel ready to, and I didn't feel confident enough to. Why would it work for me? Nothing else had. But after another few months of feeling unappreciated and unheard, I took that leap and decided now was the right time. Just before the end of the year, I rang up Liam and told him that I had decided going into the new year, I was going to join the salon and set up my own business. That would be my new project.

I opened up the business 'Josh: The Barber' in January 2018, having my own little area and have never looked back since. It started off an amazingly positive year for me, as from day one, the shop could be considered successful. I was overwhelmed with the amount of support I received from the local clients, people followed me to this venture that I never even expected to and for the first time in a very long time, I was financially stable and able to pay off some debts that I had accrued from my more difficult years. Liam managed to convince me to treat myself to a brand new black Audi A1 and it felt amazing to be able to drive an Audi, even if it was only a little A1. Not only had I tripled my income from being employed to now self-employed, but my confidence had grown significantly since opening up my own business, confidence in my work, my sexuality and in myself. If there is one thing I can say about modern society is, I may been mocked, imitated and abused as "gay", "faggot" and "queer" during my childhood years, but now I was having around hundreds of different males choosing to come to me for their haircuts and my sexuality is no bother to them, they don't care about what I am or who I love, they accept me as a person and are there for my skill and talents. The confidence that gives me each day can only be described as overwhelming. It has helped me completely accept myself for who I am and in a way, I have developed Josh The Barber as an alter-ego. He's much more confident and sociable than I am myself and he's everything I like about myself too. I am far more comfortable in that salon than I am anywhere else. I have several young boys who come in and genuinely believe my real full name is Josh The Barber and they are confused when they hear my real surname.

Opening the business was just the start of the amazing year. It was followed by the surprising news that my brother Connah and my friend Gabby were unexpectedly expecting their first child together. The pregnancy hadn't been planned as they had only been dating a short few months, but once all the family were over the shock of it, we were all over the moon that we would have another new arrival to our family. At the start of this year, I decided I was ready to and wanted to restart my trial in reducing my medication, so I could one day be medication free. My doctor accepted my request and I was reduced down to 30mg of Mirtazapine once again.

I was gutted when I realised I was going to miss Connah and Gabby's gender reveal party as Mike and I had booked a holiday to the Greek Island, Crete. But this was a holiday that would take our relationship to a whole other level. I was very suspicious of something going behind my back, and something was being planned and I admitted to my friends that I thought Mike was going to propose. However, I had been suspicious of this happening the previous year, so I wasn't a very reliable source. But the dots seemed to be joining up and clues weren't being covered up very well. The first time I noticed something suspicious happening was when Mike hired a van for a gig with his band, he told me he was struggling to get someone to pick him back up after he had returned it the next morning and I volunteered my Mum to taxi him. I went on to work that day and only on my way home during a phone call with Mike, I asked him if my Mum had collected him, he said: "No, No". So when I asked suspiciously who had, he said, "One of the cricket lads did". Again, suspiciously I asked, "Which one?" But he just shrugged it off as "Just one of the lads". I was immediately paranoid that he was acting strange and my negative mind began to wonder what was going on. My paranoia was put to an abrupt end when I got home and my Mum was cooking away in the kitchen whilst we spoke. During the conversation, she said, "Oh yeah, Mike said something about that before" and then instantly went quiet. I questioned her and asked, "When have you spoken to Mike?". She replied, "When I picked him up after he'd dropped his van off." My paranoia went to excitement straight away. He was planning something and the only thing he could possibly be planning was to propose to me. After everything I've been through, I am quite an inquisitive person, so I'm usually one step ahead if anyone is doing something without my knowledge. That and I also had told Mike I expected him to propose that year, I even made a joke that I would leave him if he failed to do so (I'd like to point out that wasn't my plan and the plan was if Mike didn't propose by the end of 2018, I would in 2019).

Another occasion that made me very suspicious of something going on behind my back was as I left work one evening. I got into my car and rang Mike as I always do. After doing this every day, you begin to know the noises of someone's house, how the audio is, the way they speak and he sounded very different. I asked him where he was and he replied that he was at home in his bedroom, but the sounds were all different. He didn't seem to be at his house, so where was he? He told me he was going to leave his house now to meet me at my own house, so I questioned if the amount of time it took him to get to mine would change, then I would know if he had been somewhere else instead of his own house. I am a massive over-thinker, as you can probably tell by now. I pulled onto the driveway at home and his car was there already. Impossible. He had said he was leaving his own house after I had gone past the turnoff for where he lived. There wasn't a chance he had only just left and arrived there before me. It was impossible for him to do so. What was going on? Why had he been there already? Was he asking my Mum and Dads permission? Was he waiting inside to propose to me there and then? As I got in, he was already sitting down with a brew and the dog Oscar sat calmly on his knee. It looked like he'd been there for definitely more than a few minutes. I thought I had it all sussed out.

Just before we were due to fly to Crete, we went out for a meal with my Dad's work staff and I was openly admitting that I believed Mike was due to propose on holiday. My Mum constantly was telling me not to get my hopes up, to not be expecting anything because he hadn't spoken to her or my Dad about it. I originally didn't believe a word she was saying, but when she expressed that she would be annoyed with Mike if he did propose without asking for their blessing, I started to doubt the trust in my knowledge. What if I got this all wrong?

We arrived in Crete on the 5th August and stayed in this beautiful hotel in the village Koutouloufari, located high up in the hills. The sun was scorching and we sat by the pool drinking cocktails. I would be reading my book or swimming in the pool and Mike was usually listening to music or reading the newspaper he'd got from a local shop—it's something he likes to do on our holidays. The first night out, I put on an outfit that I would have liked to have been proposed to and pictured in. It was a navy t-shirt with white stripes and dark chino shorts. We sat in a restaurant that overlooked the seafront, drinking wine and having a nice meal together. I wondered if this was going to be the night I got engaged. As we sat on bean bags smoking a flavoured shisha pipe, Mike told me he was tired and asked if we could make our way back to the hotel. As we opened the apartment door, I accepted that tonight wasn't going to be the night.

The next evening, I thought I would test him and asked him if I was allowed to get my own watch out of the safe—this watch he had bought me for my 21st birthday and it's something I've always treasured—but when he freely said "Yeah go for it" I was very disappointed. I had been hoping that he would tell me he would get it himself from the safe because that's where he had hidden the engagement ring, but unfortunately, as I opened the safe door, no little box and no engagement ring was hiding away. I put on my watch and felt the realisation that I may not be getting engaged on this holiday sinking in. We returned back to the apartment the second night after another lovely meal and drinks, sitting watching the ocean waves on the seafront as we talked, and I accepted that tonight wasn't the night again and the night may not be happening at all. On the third day, we walked down to the front for some lunch and sat in a restaurant that overlooked the ocean. In the distance, we spotted a small white church that seemed completely derelict and abandoned, situated out into the sea. Mike said he would like to return to this church in the evening as it was lit up during the night, but the idea of climbing along rocks to go to an unused church wasn't very appealing to me. Throughout the day, I could feel my disappointment sinking in that I had been stupidly getting excited to my friends, my family and even customers that I believed Mike was going to propose and now as I was here in Crete, I very much doubted he was going to. That night, Mike wanted to eat in the Koutouloufari village, so we stayed local to our hotel and had an outstanding meal at a small restaurant. We both drank a lot of wine and I noticed that I was also struggling to fight back the tears of disappointment as I was drinking.

"What's wrong?" He asked with a look of concern on his face.

"Nothing".

"You've got a face on you".

"I'm fine."

"Tell me, what's wrong?"

After a few attempts of him trying to get the answer out of me, I finally admitted to him, "I thought you were going to propose on this holiday, to be honest with you."

He laughed, that hurt, he laughed and said, "I've told you before I'll propose when I'm ready, and we have our own house and that."

That was it. It was official he wasn't going to propose. I was going to go back home and have to face the music and embarrassment that I had once again got it wrong. It was going to be absolutely humiliating and I only had myself to blame. We finished the rest of our meal when Mike asked if we could walk down to the front and visit the small church we had seen earlier that day. I told him I had a stomach ache and wanted to get an early night. This was a complete lie. What I really wanted was to go back to the room and sulk. Instead of getting upset at the table and embarrassing myself, I went to the toilets to text my Mum:

"Mike isn't going to propose this holiday. Tell everyone not to bring it up."

She replied, "Aww darling, I tried to warn you not to get your hopes up."

"Now he wants to go to this stupid church in the middle of the sea and I feel like I'm going to cry."

"Go to the church with him, don't forget it's his holiday too."

If my Mum had not said those words, I don't think I ever would have gone.

I'm a very stubborn person, and when I'm in that mood I was in, there is usually no backing me down. But she was right, this was Mike's holiday too and that meant we had to do things for both of us, so if Mike wanted to go visit this stupid church just because it was lit up at night, then that is what we were going to do. We walked down to the front in complete and utter silence; I complained a few times of my pretend stomach ache, hoping he would turn us back and the 25–30 minute walk was very awkward and tense. As the church came into view, lit up in the night sky, Mike asked for us to take a picture together with it in the background. In the picture, it is very obvious that I am not pleased with our plans that night. Mike, on the other hand, resembles a Cheshire Cat. As we got to the church, there were some warning signs telling tourists not to climb on the rocks, but Mike ignored them of course and had to turn on his torch on his phone and started to climb and balance along them, the open sea on the left of him and a barbed wire fence on the right. As I climbed and balanced along behind him, the waves occasionally would crash upon the rocks and spray us with saltwater and by the time we got to flat land, my clothes were clinging to me and my hair had blown everywhere by the breeze and the waves. He asked me to stand in front of the lit-up church to have a picture taken, but I wasn't feeling my best, so I refused. He asked again, but I told him I felt bloated and my clothes were clinging to me because they were wet, but he carried on and begged me to have the picture taken. He had the torch on his phone shining right on me, so I couldn't see him, only this bright white light as I stood there, forcing a smile that I didn't want to make. I saw him lower down and say something, but for a few seconds, it wasn't clear what he said. He then placed his hand out in front of the light, and I heard the words. Then, he was holding a ring in his hand and asked.

"Marry me?"

It's funny how quickly a mood can change when I get what I want. I covered my face with shock and walked a few steps back, struggling to take the moment in. I had been right along, I had doubted myself, but I had been right. There he was down on his knee with a ring in his hand asking me to marry him. The boy who had once said he didn't know if he wanted a future together, he had once said he didn't want anyone to ever know about us as a couple and now he was asking me to marry him. I knew it before, but the moment confirmed it for me, Mike loves me. I returned to him, and he had to ask again, "So will you?" while laughing and I answered smiling, laughing and crying at the same time "Yes" before we kissed and hugged and embraced each other. Within seconds he had my Mum and Dad on FaceTime, who had been ready and waiting for the news. They had known the whole time. As soon as I saw their faces, I became a blubbering mess; I could feel how proud they were from over 2400 miles away. Their son, they once worried they may not get to see grow older, had just accepted a marriage proposal and was now a fiancé. Mike told me about how he had told my Mum about his plans when she collected him from returning his hired van and the night that he had been at my house before me, his plan was he was going to ask my Dad's permission, but never managed to as my siblings were home. He told me one night when we were upstairs in my room. He went down to make us both drinks. He had snuck into the living room and showed my parents the ring and got their blessing.

We both then spent some time ringing our close family members and friends and broke the news to them all, which was a struggle as the signal wasn't great. Mike's Mum got a little confused and thought we had just gotten married when she spotted the church behind us after I held up the ring to show her, but she was absolutely thrilled when she realised we were only engaged and not yet married. Mike's Gran also got confused by Mike's statement, "Are you ok if we add another Gaskell to the family?" Her response "He can't be pregnant", as Mike had said it, I knew that it sounded stupid, but we'll put it down to too much wine, and it's now funny memory anyway. Mike's first words to his best friend were, "Fancy a stag-do mate?" No "I'm getting married" or "I've just proposed" was straight to the talk of a stag-do and I was completely ok with that. We decided to keep it off social media for a little as the pictures we had taken I wasn't best pleased with myself on. I had a very red face from crying, and my clothes were saturated from the ocean waves. We went on to celebrate drinking together. Unfortunately, I wasn't allowed to continue wearing the ring as it was far too big for my finger and Mike didn't want to risk it sliding off and losing it—he'd arranged with the jewellers to bring that one back, and I would be measured for the right size. Our plan to hold off the engagement announcement was ruined as a friend at the time posted a status on social media that basically gave away the news and other friends and customers began to message their congratulations too. I was annoyed and chose to select a picture of the two of us from the night before. I uploaded it with the caption "My Fiancé" in Greek instead of waiting to announce when we planned to. I have now grown to love the pictures of us from that night and I think it really captures the emotion of the night. It is the reality of the night and not a staged image like you usually see on social media these days. The support we received was completely overwhelming. Everyone seemed genuinely made up and happy for us. Sat in the apartment one night before we were due to go out for some food and drinks, twirling my ring around my finger and thinking, "This is it, I finally get to be happy."

Mike and I have an inside joke between us saying, "We did it". It's something we have constantly said to one another with every hurdle we have jumped over during our relationship. Once we went public with our relationship on social media, we would say "we did it" and whenever we had a moment to realise just how far we had come together, we would say to one another, "we did it." That was one of those moments, we did it, Mike. We had overcome the dark and hard times together. After returning home from Crete, straight away, I put in a request to further reduce my medication again. This would be the lowest dosage of antidepressant I had been on for a very long time. I can't say I felt amazing afterwards, but I was determined. I made a promise to myself and to Mike that I wouldn't marry him until I was completely off my medication. I wanted to have a completely clear head and my mind to be my own that day and not under the influence of a tablet.

From Crete onwards, I began to really struggle with my weight. A side effect of the Mirtazapine prescription is gaining weight and increased appetite and with the process of reducing the dosage, with each reduction, all the side effects again returned. I found myself sleepwalking on a night going downstairs, filling a large pasta bowl with different flavours of crisp, chopping up a whole block of cheddar cheese into cubes and taking this back upstairs to eat whilst asleep. I would wake up to crisp packets and chocolate wrappers at the side of my bed that I couldn't remember eating. My Mum tells me how she would come into the kitchen to check on me and would start speaking to me as I chopped up cheese, but I wouldn't answer as I was still asleep. I was slowly putting on weight, and by the end of 2018, I had gained over two and a half stone. Around the same time, I was introduced to an app on my phone that enabled me to photoshop my own pictures and make myself appear slimmer, my nose thinner and my face less round. I will openly admit that I became obsessed and didn't want a picture of me being uploaded anywhere without editing it first. I began to wear oversized hoodies to cover up the weight gain and it worked successfully for most, although one friend pointed out one time as I cut his hair that he had noticed I've put a lot of weight on, some may see this as he was being cruel, but I knew his intention and needed to hear it. This friend has been there for me through so much in my life. He's been a loyal customer and a great friend that puts me in my place when I need it. I wouldn't be where I am today without his support and I'm glad he told me that day I had put weight on, I knew it, I just wasn't ready to do anything about it.

We were having a night out for Christmas at work. The start of the night was Great Gatsby themed at a hotel, so I ordered my tuxedo that arrived two weeks before the party. Everyone kept reminding me to try it on, but I never did. I think I didn't want to realise that the tuxedo that was in my usual sizing wasn't going to fit me anymore. The night came and of course, it didn't fit me. The shirt, the blazer and the pants, none of them fit or even fasten. My Mum and Dad instantly came upstairs to help. My Dad found me a white shirt of his that he used for formal events and that fit me, he then got me his size 32 waist pants (I was usually a 28/30 waist), but they didn't fit either. Luckily he had a pair of 34 waist ones, too, that, in all honesty, only just fit. During the night, we all decided to head into the local town centre for more drinks and I realised that what I was wearing was too formal so I asked my Dad to drop me off a shirt that I had and some skinny black jeans, but as I changed into these in the hotel car park, I could feel the tightness of the shirt as my stomach bulged through and the jeans that struggled to fasten and suffocated my thighs. That was the moment I realised I had got so wrapped in what I looked like on social media that I had let how I looked in reality completely get out of control. That night, I voluntarily decided to do cocaine again. This was the first sign for me to realise that I wasn't in the best frame of mind.

I would love to say take a look on social media at how I used to look back then, but all these images of myself from that time are the photoshopped ones—I haven't deleted them from my social media as it's a memory to me now of how low I once felt about myself.

As the year was coming to an end, I was down to the lowest dosage of medication and taking it less frequently than daily, the end of the process was in sight and there was no event like what had happened in Manchester coming along to stop me now. The month of December is always a busy one in the barbering industry and this was my first Christmas being self-employed. I had been operating on an appointment system since earlier in the year and I had a lot more control over the intake of clients, but I had chosen to work long, hard, and extra hours to fit as many people as I could in. This wasn't for financial reasons. I was in the best place financially I had been in for years, but I've always had a pressure of feeling that I don't want to let people down, so I repeatedly say yes and choose to open earlier, close later and work extra days as Christmas approached. Six days before Christmas, Mike and I were enjoying a night together at my house and of course, we enjoyed ourselves the way couples do, but as it came to an end, I suddenly got an intense pain in the back of my head that felt like someone had just thrown a brick directly into the back of my head causing blood to run down. I grabbed my head as I screamed out in pain, feeling for the blood, but there was no blood there and as I went to look at my hand, I realised my vision had completely gone. I could only see darkness. I shut my eyes tight, even with Mike demanding me to open them. I thought I had gone blind and I didn't want to realise that I had, so I kept them shut and started focusing on my breathing, trying to calm myself down. The pain stayed for a while and I refused for Mike to go and tell my Mum, I knew that she would panic, so I decided to sleep it off instead. When I woke up the next morning, I didn't feel quite right and the pain was still there, although it wasn't as intense as the night before.

    Before he left for work, Mike insisted that I rang the NHS Advice Line before I drove to work in case it was something dangerous. I thought they were going to tell me to take some painkillers or anti-inflammatories. I did not expect them to tell me they were sending an ambulance as soon as they could. I begged the advisor to leave it as I had a very busy day at work that day, but she insisted that I needed to get this checked out before attempting to drive to work or even working. I felt devastated that I was going to have to cancel people's appointments just before Christmas, so I cancelled just the morning appointments, hoping that I could return to work for the afternoon. I went to my Mum and cried, telling her an ambulance was coming for me; she was in complete shock as she had no idea anything had even happened to me. We decided it would be quicker for my

Mum to drive me up to the hospital instead of waiting for an ambulance, and Mike met us there too. Blood tests were taken, and a cannula was put in my arm before I was sent down for a CT scan on my brain. After some time waiting, the doctor returned and asked me to go down for another CT scan to be done, but this time a fluid of dye ran through my body—the sensation of the fluid was so strange and I felt like I had wet myself in front of everyone.

    I admitted to myself that I wouldn't be returning to work that day, so I had to cancel the remaining appointments for the rest of the day. The doctor came to me and suggested that I have a lumbar puncture done to rule out any further bleed on the brain. I had already been told the procedure was extremely painful but was happy to have it done, but when the doctor explained that it would only be able to be done the next day, this was when like I explained in a previous chapter, the memory of the incident with the doctor when I was a young teen took a few steps forward into my conscious mind and I refused to stay over in the hospital and to wait any longer, demanding the procedure to be done either that day or not at all. Mike and my Mum were both angry with me for being so dismissive of the seriousness of what could be happening, but I passed it off as I needed to get back to work for my clients and didn't want to let people down. This was true, but there was also the fear of being in a hospital on my own without my Mum there to protect me. Fortunately, a very kind doctor came in on his day off and successfully completed the procedure the same day, so after laying flat for 2 hours afterwards, I was able to be home by 9 pm with strict orders to rest. I didn't rest. I returned to work the very next day and worked the next five days, doing even more hours to fit in clients that I had had to cancel. I felt like I hit rock bottom and I looked and felt horrendously ill. Looking in the mirror, I felt disgusted with what I saw and how I felt. To stop myself from letting other people down, I let myself down.

    Christmas Eve night, I arranged with James to meet him for a drink in our local town, at the place where everyone we had gone to school with would be. I hadn't been in the previous years due to the conflict that had happened with Sarah's cousin, but this year I decided it was time I returned to our usual tradition with my friend. As I drank my first drink, I knew I didn't feel too great. My body felt weak, my head was pounding, and my eyesight was delayed as I looked around the venue. I was talking to some girls I had gone to school with about my visit to the hospital when I was informed that Sarah had walked in. I looked over and spotted her standing there with her sister and wondered what I should do. I wanted to go over and say hello or even just walk past and smile, but she had blocked all contact with me and made it clear she didn't want a hello or a smile, so I walked past and ignored her, deciding to leave and go home. If I would have been feeling better, I probably would have stuck it out longer and hoped to have a conversation with her that night, but I was just far too drained to even attempt building a collapsing bridge. I've always been ashamed of myself since I had gained weight as I wasn't looking great at all and I was physically and mentally exhausted. Nobody wants to see their ex when they are looking their worst, no matter what you have gone through. So if the real Sarah or her sister is still reading this book, I'm sorry for blanking you that night, I just wasn't feeling great and it's not the way I wanted to feel if I was going to try to resolve our differences.

The new year came in and I was excited for the possibilities to come. Mike and I had decided a while back to start saving for a house together, and the new year meant we would start looking at some properties and hopefully find the right one. But I had also made another promise to myself that year, after standing next to a heavily pregnant Gabby as she carried my nephew for a photograph together, there was an obvious weight gain for both of us. Gabby, of course, had quite an obvious reason for her weight gain. She was nine months pregnant. On the other hand, I was not and was disgusted with the image I saw of myself. Even wearing an oversized jumper, I still looked larger than ever. I would love to go on to say that I spent the next year going to the gym and getting in better shape, but I didn't do that. Instead, I went to put even more weight on, eat a hell of a lot more than usual, exercise less and photoshop my pictures on social media more and more. Special moments were ruined by how I viewed myself in the pictures. On the 27th January 2019, I held my newborn nephew Chester Luke Finch in my arms. In the photograph, all I can see is how my cheeks are bulging up against my face and my neck had grown in size. All these things that could be altered by photoshopping them out, though. It became the normal practice for me to heavily edit my photos before uploading them to social media. A small break away to the Lake District with Mike, before we moved into our own house, I spent half the afternoon photoshopping and editing the pictures before uploading them to my social media and then seeing the unedited versions and hating myself for how I looked. During that break away, thoughts of self-harming started to creep back into my mind and I knew my mental health was slipping and I was losing control, but I refused to go back on any form of medication.

However, buying the house was a massive distraction for me and kept my brain off my mental health for some time. We originally put an offer in on another house and had to jump many hurdles trying to obtain a mortgage, as most lenders didn't seem to trust me for being self-employed only short term and only having a smaller deposit. As everything eventually came into play after some very stressful weeks and with help from my parents, we lost that house. The surveyors went to the property, but the current rental tenants refused them entry and the owner of the house decided to accept their lower offer to buy the property as the easiest option. We were completely devastated. We had started to plan our lives here, having discussions about how we were going to decorate each room, what jobs we would do, the house, etc. This was going to be our home, and we had lost it with no chance of getting it back. I remember sitting in the dark in my bedroom at home and my Mum telling me there would be other houses, better houses and they would be the right one and I felt like she didn't understand, nobody understood, that was going to be our house and after all the stress we had gone through trying to get a mortgage for it, we had the opportunity taken from us, unfairly and unprofessionally. Again, it's frightening how much a mood can change because, within a day of losing that house, I found another property for sale on the next estate. Mike didn't seem as excited for this viewing as it was a newer house, and he originally had stated he didn't want to purchase a new build property, even if it was over 15 years old. This house was very tucked away and private, so we struggled to find it on the street at first, but eventually, we pulled onto the driveway and I got that feeling that everybody told me I would get. I knew this was going to be our house. I loved the privacy of the property. It really drew me in, of course, there were things I wasn't in love with, but the privacy was perfect for me. Our offer was eventually accepted and three months later, four days after my 24th birthday, we moved into our first home together. This was definitely another "we did it" moment.

Living together was definitely a learning experience. We both do things that irritate one another. We've both been raised differently, so we both have certain ways of doing things around the house that the other doesn't seem to understand, but I can honestly say living together has poured concrete into our relationship. It has tested us and we have survived all the hurdles life has thrown at us. So we decided it was time for another challenge, a challenge we had both been excited for, a challenge we had spoken about repeatedly before we had even thought of buying a house. We decided it was time to become parents for a dog. After falling in love with one of my customer's dogs, a black Cocker Spaniel, we finally found the perfect chocolate brown Working Cocker Spaniel puppy for us from a private breeder in Salford and on the 7th July, we brought home little Albus, named after Albus Dumbledore from Harry Potter. To say I am obsessed with Albus is an understatement. We see him as our child. We don't have our children and don't plan to, so our dogs are our children to us, even if others don't understand that. Everyone at work laughed about how I would find any excuse to talk about Albus and how excited I was, counting down the days until we finally got to bring him home. I feel sorry for the breeders as I went every weekend until we brought him home, four weekends in a row. However, Albus had his issues when we got him home, he was very small and his digestive system wasn't working correctly and we became worried that we wouldn't have him for very long, but we managed to love and care for him enough and he loved and cared for us back on a whole other level.

As all the distractions came to a close, my ongoing problems became apparent. I had had thoughts of self-harming for months and I was starting to lose control of my temper and mood swings. I became snappy and argumentative with Mike for any small thing, I wasn't sleeping at night, and my quality of work was starting to be affected. I decided I needed to see a therapist again. I had seen a private therapist the year previous and the sessions were enough for that time, but I didn't feel it was effective enough to return the following year. So this was when I had my first appointment with Catherine Shaw. I will openly admit, at first, I didn't think these sessions would be successful, as Catherine is very different to the other therapist I have seen, but she provided me with some amazing CBT skills and made it clearer to understand than anyone else had previously.

A real turning point for me to get myself sorted and in better health was whilst at my nephew Chester's christening. Gabby and my brother had asked me to be his godfather and I felt truly honoured. I bought a suit specially for the occasion and on the day I felt good about myself. However, as the day drew to a close, a family member made a comment that I was looking "big" and had "put some weight on" and I instantly felt disgusted. I sat and tried to distract myself, I tried to practice the skills I had been taught, but I repeated the comments over and over again to myself until I felt like I was physically going to throw up and began shaking. That day I debated making myself sick, but I knew how dangerous that path was to go down and instead asked Mike if we could leave. We left instantly and I cried before I even managed to get back to the car. I threw the suit in the bin that night and promised myself that I would have lost weight the next time I saw that family member.

CHAPTER TWELVE

Before the end of that year, Mike and I took a trip to Anglesey, North Wales. It is a place that is very special to him and his family and we had come to love together. This was Albus's first family trip here and I was really looking forward to some downtime to relax in a small village on the coast called Benllech. It's a stunning location and a place we visit quite frequently now and as laughable as it may seem, the dogs absolutely loved it here. The walks along the beach and along the coastal front of Moelfre were really what I needed to give my head that mental break from the chaos of overthinking. Everything had been so fast-paced for so long, and I needed room to breathe and the break from reality gave me that. Ever since we had become engaged, we had been discussing some wedding plans. Originally, I wanted to keep the wedding between the two of us, to go to an office and sign some paperwork and the deal be done, but Mike knew it would devastate both of our Mums if we got married without them. We even planned on a Vegas wedding at one point, I joked about how Britney Spears had got married in a hoodie and ripped jeans, and I would do the same. Jon Bon Jovi had got married in Vegas too, so the idea that both our favourite artists had done this seemed like fate, but my Mum's disgust of that idea threw it straight out the window and in all honesty, I'm very relieved we didn't do that. We had started to plan to return to Crete to look at possible wedding venues and then return to be married there the following year. The wedding plans went from having a small event to having around 60 guests. Once we were having more and more discussions about the wedding plans with other family members and friends, more ideas and decisions were being made. The wedding was going to have a black and white theme, the males of the family all in black and the females of the family in white. There was going to be a formal meal after the ceremony and then we would rent a private pool with a private bar at the hotel and have a party there. Upon returning home to England, we were going to have a party of over 200 guests to celebrate the wedding with them all who couldn't attend the wedding in Crete. I have no idea how it went from being a small intimate service between the two of us to this big ceremony, but it wasn't the day I wanted at all, it was the perfect and ideal wedding for other people, but the thought of walking down the aisle in front of all those people just filled me with anxiety, not excitement. During our break away to the Lake District before we moved into our home, I confessed to Mike that I didn't want the wedding we were planning and we decided with the upcoming house move that we would put the wedding plans on the back burner and we only discussed it every so often. We did book a holiday to Crete for the following year with the intention of looking at some venues whilst over there, but there was no plan to have lots of guests and themes anymore.

    I asked my Dad quite early on into wedding planning to be my best man and Mike and I decided to ask our Mums if they would walk us down the aisle. The video footage of my Mum receiving her card to ask this is iconic—and features lots of tears.

    Just before the trip to Anglesey, later on that year, I thought of the idea of having a secret wedding. After watching Britney Spears marry Kevin Federline on their reality show, I had always been intrigued by the idea. The guests all turned up to the venue believing it was an engagement party and discovered as they arrived that it was, in fact, the wedding. I told Mike about my idea, but he just rolled his eyes and shrugged it off as a silly idea. We attended the wedding reception of his childhood friend together the night before we left for Anglesey and on the way home from this beautiful evening, I voiced my idea once again to Mike. He seemed less reluctant than he originally did, but he expressed he would like to have a stag do with his friends and questioned if the wedding was kept a secret if that would be possible. We decided to leave the conversation for now, or Mike decided to leave it, and I just gave up trying. But during the break in Anglesey, it became heavily discussed between the two of us. Mike reluctantly, however I could see that he was warming to the idea of having this small secret wedding. He did admit that he liked the idea of having a party of all our friends and family together after the wedding so we could reveal it to them there.

In a small pub in Moelfre, we decided to go for it and I started to look up small wedding venues in our local town, selecting a very small venue called The Lodge that was situated in a park in the town centre. We went through some possible dates. I was really pushing for February, but Mike insisted that we wait a little longer and we went for April during the Easter holidays so he would be off work for it. We finally settled on April 17th 2020 and were to have the surprise party disguised as our engagement party the following weekend on April 24th. We texted each of our immediate families and asked them to save the date and so the excitement for us all began. Planning was in full force and I had the biggest project to focus on and the secret was revealed to those who needed to know. Mike really struggled to pick between his friends who he wanted to have as his best man, so he eventually chose two of his closest friends. I had already asked my Dad and then I asked James, who had stood by me throughout all my dark times and believed me the second I told him my truth—we had always said in high school we would be one another's best man, and now here we were, it was becoming a reality. In complete honesty, even though it was my idea, I wasn't the best at keeping this a secret. I got drunk at our Christmas Work's Night and slipped up and told my best friend Laura, but she was absolutely amazing and never told anyone. She didn't even tell me that I had told her for some time. I had to tell my friend Liam in the very early stages of planning just to make sure he could be there.

As the year 2020 started, I had officially stopped taking my antidepressants and we finally selected a stunning venue to have the wedding reception. We asked Mike's sister Natalie to be in charge of the dessert catering and she created a beautiful dessert cart. She had started her own dessert business and this was going to be a great opportunity for her to promote her talents. Mike had chosen and booked a really good DJ / Host that we had seen at Mike's childhood friend's wedding and I had booked a talented saxophone player that

Liam's girlfriend recommended. We planned on revealing the wedding to our friends and family through a video, after my Dad had given a speech. I made the first half of the video quite early on using a collection of photos and videos from the years we had been together over some beautiful instrumental music. I asked Mike to record the song 'Love Me Like You Do' by Ellie Goulding as this was one of our songs. I wanted this song to be in the background of the video as the photos and videos from the wedding day played. He only went into the recording studio with his former bandmate to record the song a month before the wedding was due, which sent my stress levels through the roof. Although I was looking forward to the wedding reception with all our friends and family, the thought of it all was giving me massive anxiety attacks. I was dreading the moment everyone turned to look for Mike and me once they realised what was happening and then dancing in front of everybody. We had decided quite early on into our wedding planning process that we didn't want to do the first dance together. It just didn't represent the way we are as a couple. We decided instead that we were going to ask our Mums to dance with us. Originally this was a dance to the Celine Dion cover of "Power Of Love", as the original "Power Of Love" was played at my Grandad's funeral. However, Mike's sister Natalie suggested a beautiful song by Callum Scott called "No Matter What". The first time I listened to this song, I was driving in the car on my way home from work and I cried my eyes out. The lyrics seemed to be telling my story perfectly from hating myself, having my friends turn their back on me and my amazing relationship with my Mum, always being there loving and supporting me. I played the song for Mike and he agreed this would be the song we danced with our Mums to. Every time I thought about that moment of dancing with my Mum leading up to the wedding day, I'd get very emotional.

By the end of February, I had done everything I needed to do, even down to picking my suit. I already knew that I had wanted a light grey skinny fitted suit so with my best men, my Dad and James, went to the Trafford Centre to find this suit that I had in mind but never saw. We went to a few different stores, some with extremely expensive suits but none of them seemed to be the right one. I didn't feel like any of them fit me, looked right or suited me. After some browsing, my suit ended up being the least expensive out of all of them. I purchased it from Top Man and I found the perfect suit that I had been envisioning. As soon as I tried this suit on I knew it was the right one for me—the biggest bonus of that day was I found out that I was back down to a size 30 waist pants. Since the beginning of that year, I had started a fasting diet and if I'm honest, the weight was rapidly dropping off me. I won't lie and say I wasn't completely made up when people started to notice and I started to get comments at work about my weight loss. Besides regular visits to the gym, the fasting diet was slowly getting me back into shape and losing all the weight I had put on over the past year or more. I will admit it did become an obsession for me to get to the slimmest I've ever been ready for the wedding. Whilst I was swimming in the pool at the gym I would repeat in my head the comments made to me by all the people who were noticing I'd lost weight. I had to have an operation on my stomach in January and I was much more concerned with how quick I would be able to get back into the gym than I was about the healing process and the success of the surgery. At each appointment with the nurse to change dressings and check on the wound, I constantly would ask, "how many more weeks until I go to the gym?". Not many people know that around this time, I did become dangerously close to going down the dark path of starting to make myself vomit each time that I ate. I felt like because I couldn't exercise that I needed to do something to stop any slight weight gain from happening. I was only having one meal a day due to the intermittent fasting, but even that one meal was causing me worry and anxiety. My Mum became very concerned that I was losing too much weight and very concerned that I was becoming too skinny and I can't say that I didn't enjoy her worry either. It meant everything was working. There were nights I would sit on the couch with Mike after finishing our tea and would try to think of ways I could go and make myself sick without him realising. Fortunately, I failed to come up with any ways to sneak around him for this and I am proud to say I never went down the dangerous road.

Everything was ready for the perfect day. But that's not our story. That's not what happened. In all honesty, how could I have expected it to? Had my life beforehand not taught me that I never seemed to get things easily? Had all the battles that I had fought in and all the hurdles that I jumped taught me nothing? That I always had to win the battles and jump over hurdles to get what I wanted or happiness. I laugh now at how I expected that perfect day to go ahead as planned, but April 17th 2020, was unfortunately not the day I got married.

In January 2020, the first cases of Coronavirus were reported in the UK. By the end of February, it had increased to having over 25 cases. I heard about the virus's rapid spread on the news and became really concerned that it may affect our wedding reception but didn't worry over the wedding service as we were having less than 20 guests anyway. I was cutting my brother Adam's hair in the salon one day and I expressed my worries about the virus. Both he and Liam started to laugh and reassured me that the government wouldn't be bothered about our party in comparison to football games and racing events. But by March, after the first death with Covid, I started to really panic that this was becoming more serious than anyone had planned. Fortunately, we were distracted from all the chaos going on in the world and from all the negativity as Mike and I went to view another puppy. I spotted this beautiful little black female Cocker Spaniel on a group page on Facebook. The post explained that she had been returned to the breeder after the family had her for only one day. I have always felt extremely sorry for dogs that get returned through no fault of their own and worried how confused it makes them. I spent the whole day trying to convince Mike that this little puppy was meant to be ours and then I finally cracked him. We went to see her in Salford the following day and picked her up the following weekend. We decided to name her Aurora. I originally wanted to call her Ariana as in the Harry Potter novels, Albus' sister is named Ariana. However, Mike knew people would assume it was after Ariana Grande, so instead, we found a list of all Harry Potter character's names beginning with the letter "A" and selected the name Aurora. I could already picture my little niece Evie calling her "Rora" instead and to this day, she still does. We introduced little Aurora to Albus and the two of them instantly became best friends. She showed him she was boss straight away and she fitted in with our little family, although she didn't give us much choice as she is very forceful with her affection of kisses to those she loves.

Through the middle of March, the awareness of COVID-19 was completely unavoidable, everybody was talking about it and rumours were spreading of a pending national lockdown. I began to worry, not just for the wedding plans but for my family's safety, as the statistics began to rise. My Dad had had his heart attack a few years back. Would he be classed as vulnerable? Mike's Grandparents had to go into shielding now to lower their risk of catching the virus and we knew that we were definitely not going to continue with the wedding without them being there. The wedding was looking very unlikely, but what about my business? On an online group of other barbers and other business owners were voluntarily closing their doors for safety. I thought this seemed ridiculous at first, but as time went on some of the barbers in the group became verbally abusive to those who hadn't closed their businesses yet. This included to myself when I declared that I was going to be working one more week before I voluntarily closed my business down. I was labelled "selfish", "disgusting" and told I "don't care about killing" my family, all because financially, my partner and I needed me to continue working. On Sunday, March 22nd, I had a discussion with Laura. She had decided for her child and her own safety. She was closing her business down, I also spoke to a local council member and they advised that I did close down too. I decided to voluntarily close my business down, making Saturday, March 21st, my last working day, hopefully to return for May 1st. However, the following day the UK went into national lockdown, and our wedding venue informed us that our wedding had to be postponed to July.

I sat there feeling very sorry for myself because my wedding had been cancelled, but weddings could happen when everything reopened, they could be easily rearranged, but there were those who couldn't attend loved one's funerals, which is far worse and I believe the cruellest part of the pandemic. A funeral couldn't be postponed or wait until everything reopened and those rare moments that you can never get back. We accepted that April 17th would no longer be our wedding date and arranged with the venue, the wedding reception venue and everything else that we would move the date to July 11th instead. We honestly thought by then that the whole pandemic would be over, the country would be back functioning and be able to continue as we planned. On a socially distanced walk with Gabby over the lockdown, we discussed the new wedding date and I admitted to her that I had no attachment to the new date and I didn't believe it would even happen then.

We received very little financial support in this lockdown, but we were grateful to have a payment break from our mortgage and my car finance bill. Luckily, I managed to save up some savings pre-pandemic for the wedding and we were able to survive on them along with the refunds for the holidays to New York and Crete that we had planned. These would have been our honeymoons. Mike was working days and had reduced to 2 days a week with the rest of the weekdays he was working from home and for the first time in our relationship, we were spending a lot of time together, something that we were not used to at all. If you would have asked me at the time if I was glad the wedding had been delayed, I would have become very irritated and annoyed and thought you were an insensitive arsehole for asking me such a thing, but looking back now, I believe we needed this time, more time with one another before we made that commitment to marry one another. We had more conversations, learnt more about one another, irritated each other and argued together as the lockdown era developed and I genuinely believe that we came out of that lockdown a stronger partnership. We needed it. During the lockdown, we had some conversations where I learnt some things about Mike that I had no idea of before. Things that had happened years before we met and he had decided to keep from me, the things that I found out didn't jeopardise our relationship, but the lying about them did. After an argument, I decided to spend a night back at my parent's home and debated if the wedding was the right thing to do. I knew that Mike loved me and that I loved him and that's all I needed to know to decide to move on from this. I think with the deceit I had experienced before I met Mike, I really do struggle with handling lies and still to this day, so it made me question our relationship, but Mike isn't Charlie. He's Mike. He doesn't deserve to be punished for things Charlie did to me and I knew relationships take work and lessons and this was a big lesson for both of us.

When April 17th came around, I got up in the morning and stupidly decided to listen to our wedding playlist that I had made of all the songs that were going to be a part of our day whilst I washed the dishes. I stood and thought about what should have been happening on that day, the excitement we all would have been feeling and compared it to being in a lockdown and unable to even see my own parents as we were not in their social bubble. I was absolutely devastated and I cried a lot that day. We comforted one another that day and kept ourselves busy and joined in with what everyone else seemed to be doing this lockdown, and that was painting the garden fences. Instead of walking down the aisle holding my Mum's hand and marrying the love of my life, I was crouched down in the garden painting stupid garden fences.

Halfway through the lockdown, I knew I needed to keep myself busy as I'm not a person who copes well without having a routine and distractions and I knew that if I continued the way I was doing that I could end up in a mentally dark place again, so I decided that I wanted to help others with their own mental health issues and I enrolled on an online counselling course. I threw myself straight into studying, doing all the reading, taking the notes, writing assignment after assignment and getting amazing results back with great feedback. I felt great. I am very proud to say that I completed a potentially two-year counselling course in just eight weeks, achieved full marks on most of my assignments and achieved a Level 4 TQUK in Counselling & Cognitive Behaviour Therapy. I loved how it made me feel and I became excited to eventually help others get through their dark times too. I decided I wanted to continue to do counselling as a part-time role alongside my barbering and hoped one day to become a full-time counsellor.

I started to meditate twice a day, practiced daily yoga and frequently went running, tracking my time and distance and uploaded it to social media, another thing everybody else seemed to be doing in the lockdown. I took part in online exercise classes that a friend was leading as I wanted to make sure I kept my weight off for the wedding and wanted to carry on getting compliments that I had lost more weight. I did lose more weight during the lockdown and it started to become a concern for myself and my Mum that the suit I had bought back in February would no longer fit me.

We received an email from our wedding venue in June to inform us that our wedding in July had been postponed again. I can't say I wasn't expecting this news, but it was still heartbreaking to hear that we got so close to the date we would be married to have it pulled from underneath us once again. We did have some good news, the government had confirmed that my barbering business would be allowed to reopen on July 4th, but unfortunately, weddings would still not be permitted. The next possible date for us to get married was October, as Mike needed to be off work. We weren't given very much choice of dates understandably, as many others were rescheduling their own weddings too. We finally selected Saturday, October 10th. This date was my brother Connah's birthday too, so I rang him first to make sure that we had his blessing to do so first. Thank you for that, Connah.

Returning to work was really daunting after having so much time off, more time off than I had ever had since leaving school. I felt like I had changed as a person a lot during the lockdown. I continued my meditation, exercise regimes and studying. I even became interested in crystals and their uses, so going back to a very busy lifestyle of working 50 hours a week became overwhelming. I once described the return to work as like "Moving from New York to the peaceful Lake District and now I'm moving back to the chaos of New York again". I became scared that I wouldn't be able to keep myself calm without the routines I had put in place. They were helping my mental health, I was in the best place mentally and in the best shape physically that I had been in for years and I was scared of jeopardising that. Fortunately, I was back into the swing of things within a few weeks of returning to work. I did have to wear a lot of PPE including a facial mask, a facial visor, a disposable apron, disposable gloves and I also had to provide facial masks and disposable gowns for the clients too, it was like being back in New York but looking more like a surgeon, not a barber.

Shortly after I returned back to work, one morning I received a message from a customer informing me that my shop sign had been graffitied through the night. The graffiti read the words "Gay Boy". I went straight into autopilot mode and made the phone calls to have the graffitied sign taken down immediately. Liam reacted so supportive and really quickly and had the sign removed rapidly. My parents and Mike insisted that I report this to the police and I honestly was shocked at how seriously they took the abuse, it is a hate crime and they did everything they could to catch the culprit. Unfortunately, although we believe we know who did the damage, without enough evidence, we weren't able to prove it, but in my eyes, I still won. I arrived on that day with a fully booked diary and laughed the matter off with my customers. That is what I do; this is what I will always do in serious situations. I will laugh no matter how much things are getting to me. Was I hurt by the words? Yes! Did I let it get to me? A little! Do I care that some low life doesn't like that I am gay? Not at all. Luckily, we live in a society today where homophobic people are becoming the minority and differences are being publicly accepted. I am very broad-minded and I do not expect everyone to agree with my lifestyle or my choices in relationships, but if an individual doesn't agree that I am married to a male, it doesn't automatically wrap up our marriage certificate, so I won't allow them to damage my feelings either.

Everything seemed to be going great after I returned to work, the figures of daily deaths and infections were decreasing and the chances of the wedding and reception going ahead for October seemed more probable. Until September.

As the resurgence of the COVID-19 spread began, more and more restrictions were being reinstated and we all began to worry again that the wedding would be cancelled for a third time. My Mum constantly reminded me not to get my hopes up, but I wanted to do everything I could to try and stay positive. I believed if I stayed positive, there could be a chance that the wedding may happen. A month before the wedding reception was due, I rang the venue to check what restrictions they had in place and how they felt about having the party of over 200 guests. However, the restrictions stated that there could be no more than 60 people in their venue. There also could be no dancing, no singing and no standing up or moving around. It didn't sound anything at all like the party that we planned, so it was decided to cancel the wedding reception and just focus on the wedding service itself if that was even possible to happen. Some people questioned why we didn't just cancel the wedding altogether until the following year—the main reason for that was because we wanted to make sure Mike's Grandparents would be present at the wedding. Mike's Grandad was turning 90 years old, and his Gran in her 70s. Time is so precious at that age and after my experience of losing three of my grandparents in my teens, I very much understood that Mike didn't want to wait any longer and wanted to make sure they were here to see him get married.

    We continued the build-up to the wedding day as if the wedding was definitely happening even though the potential of it happening was becoming very unlikely. During a visit to the Trafford Centre with my Mum one day, the aim of the day to find her a hat or hair accessory for the wedding, my Mum was becoming more stressed than I was, but her way of dealing with the stress was to verbally prepare for another cancellation whereas my own way was to try to remain positive and manifest that it would happen. I got so frustrated with her in the car on the way to the Trafford Centre as she said, "It's probably pointless even doing this, it's probably not going to happen" I knew she was trying to help me by not getting my hopes up and having them be crushed again. I know my Mum wants the best for me, she wants the best for all of us and she was really concerned that I wasn't getting the day I deserved or wanted, but what she didn't realise was that as long as at the end of that day I was married to Mike, by that time I no longer cared about how it happened. I should have been married for six months and I wasn't waiting any longer for it to happen. My Mum was a stressful pain leading up to the wedding day, she worried about every little detail, such as which sides of the room she would be on and if Mike's Mum wanted to wear a flower, as she didn't, but she didn't want to not match, but I know all her stressing was just because she wanted the best for me, but God you pissed me off at times, Mum! Even with all the stress, we had such a nice day together once the shopping began. We laughed and got excited together and I did my best to try make her laugh and smile—even walking around the shop wearing a big wedding hat for a while until she noticed. We went for some lunch at the wedding breakfast venue and whilst we were there and viewing the room we both started to get really excited, especially Mum. On the way home, we listened to the playlist of our wedding songs in the car and we cried together.

Two weeks before the wedding was due to take place, I stood at work cutting a client's hair as an announcement from the government was on the radio about further restrictions in the UK. This list included only 15 guests permitted to attend weddings—this caused a problem as we had 16 adults and two infants as our wedding party. The minute I finished the client's hair, I ran to the toilet and rang the wedding venue, they hadn't even heard the announcement, so I had to speak to a manager regarding the latest update, she returned with some more bad news, as although the new restrictions had stated that 15 guests could attend weddings, the venue itself was only allowing 6 guests to attend. We were already having a very small wedding, but how on earth were we meant to reduce the number of guests down to 6! As I came off the phone I was physically sick into the toilet and then I dialled Mike's number, I didn't expect him to pick up, but when he did I just started to cry down the phone to him telling him the frustrating bad news, he told me to leave work and meet him at home so we could sort this together. I cancelled my appointments for the day and returned home. We only had a few options, to either rearrange our whole wedding day again, to cancel it all together or persevere and go through with whatever plans we could. We considered venue change but there were complications then with our wedding license, so it was then decided that we would continue with the day as planned and have only our parents inside the venue. Our remaining guests were to stand outside the venue and watch the ceremony through the open glass windows—we prayed for good weather that day.

The week before the wedding, whilst at work, I started to feel unwell. I felt faint and nauseous, and when I arrived home during my dinner break, I became really dizzy and suffered extreme lightheadedness. I had to cancel my remaining appointments for that day and did my best to try to sleep off the unwell feeling. I started panicking that I may have contracted Coronavirus a week before the wedding day. I woke up the next day feeling incredibly worse. I couldn't even lift my head off the pillow without going dizzy and feeling nauseous, so I had no choice but to cancel my appointments once again and try to sleep it off. I didn't move out of bed for the full day, mostly in fear that I could collapse and injure myself if I attempted to walk downstairs. On Saturday morning, I felt a touch better but not good. Mike and my Mum decided it was best for me to take the day off and relax as much as I could to be ready to return to work the following week and be better for the wedding. Some may question why I didn't go for a Covid test and I would explain that I didn't have the main three symptoms that they were advising if you had, to go and be tested but the main reason I never went for a Covid test was because I was absolutely terrified of the result coming back positive and having to cancel our wedding yet again. I reassured myself that I didn't have the Covid symptoms of temperature, cough and loss of taste and smell, so I couldn't have had it.. By Tuesday morning, I was back to my full health, and nothing was standing in our way now of finally getting married.

Up until the night before, I wouldn't accept that this wedding was going to go ahead. I went to work as of normal the day before, still keeping it a secret from most of what was happening the following day (by this point, we had told the majority of our close friends and family as we knew our original plan to reveal the wedding at the fake engagement party would no longer be going ahead) and trying my best to not to get too excited or my hopes up about it. It was only when I pulled up onto my parent's driveway after dropping my own car off at the hotel we would be staying in for the wedding night that I took a deep breath and accepted that I was getting married in the morning. I drank a couple of glasses of wine with my Mum and Dad, had a face mask and my Mum even treated me to a pedicure as all three of us started to get excited that the wedding was officially going ahead. I woke up in the morning with a slight hangover from the wine and the nerves well and truly kicked in. The day felt alien to me, I was really tired from a night of disturbed sleep and I wasn't sure what to do with myself until the afternoon. I visited my brother with my Dad for his birthday whilst my Mum went for her hair to be done and when I returned to their home, there was nothing else to do other than get ready for the service. Mike came to collect the buttonhole flowers for himself and his best men as I was getting ready and I sat at the top of the stairs hidden away, listening to him. I couldn't wait to see him later.

Putting on my suit was a very surreal moment for me. I stood in the spare bedroom of my parent's house (this room once belonged to my brother Adam) and as I walked out of the room, there was a framed picture on the wall facing the door, the picture was a drawing of my grandparents holding my niece and nephew as they sadly never got to. All of their faces were smiling at me, their eyes on me and I looked to my Gran, my Grandad Tommy and my Nan and said to them, "I hope I've made you proud", just wishing that they could have been there that day. I think I spent most of that morning with tears in my eyes. It could have been due to the lack of sleep, the slight headache from the wine or the fact that the day was just a very emotional one. I came downstairs to both my parents dressed, my Mum looking absolutely stunning in her custom made dress, her hat clipped perfectly in place and my Dad was looking incredibly dapper in his dark grey best man suit with our waistcoats, ties, shoes and belt matching. I'm incredibly proud to be their son and on this day, I could see in their eyes how incredibly proud they are to be my parents. In the morning, I was panicking about anything that could potentially have called the wedding off. I even had my Mum keep checking my temperature before we went to the venue in case I was running a fever when we got there and then they would have refused to marry us. Thankfully, there was no temperature, and after waiting on James, my brother Connah and my nephew Chester to arrive, we sneakily climbed into my Dad's car, hiding away from the neighbours and we were on the way to the venue.

The original plan was that I would get to the venue first, go inside and have my meeting with the registrar as we waited for Mike to arrive with his best men and our other guest. However, my party was running late and Mike arrived at the park earlier than he had planned, which was before me. This completely stressed me out. I demanded he move away from the front of the venue so he couldn't see me as I walked in. He waited at the opposite end of the park, tucked away whilst his best men kept watch and waited for everyone else to arrive. Knowing that he'd at least turned up helped calm my nerves a little—at least I wasn't going to be abandoned at the altar. As soon as I pulled up, I rushed straight inside the venue, not waiting for anyone else, my Mum following behind me, rushing in her heels. As I walked into the room that we were to be married in, the nerves kicked in big time. By the window stood looking in were my brothers, Rachael, my niece, my nephew, Natalie and Kieran and I could see walking up behind them Mike's parents with his grandparents, just seeing everyone all dressed up, looking their smartest and all here for us was so overwhelming to me that I couldn't stand being stood there in the room and being the centre of attention. I knew how much this day meant to my family, especially after everything they had watched me go through. They were so proud to stand there and watch their son and their little brother get married. The photographer captured a moment of my emotion (it has just been chosen to be on the front cover of this book). I turned to my Mum and asked if we could wait outside in the corridor as I had got completely overwhelmed with nerves, excitement, anxiety and happiness and could feel myself starting to cry. There was so much happiness. I sat down in the corridor, shaking, my legs twitching, crying, and I started to question myself. I sat there and I thought, "Is this what I want?" Did I want to get married? Did I want to make this commitment to him? Did I want to spend the rest of my life with him? Was this marriage going to work? What if it didn't? What if I just turned around now and decided to cancel? What was everyone else thinking? Did people think we should be getting married? Did anyone think we shouldn't? Did Mike's family really want Mike to marry me? All of this went through my head as I sat there in that corridor holding my Mum's hand. The registrar told me that Mike had arrived and was in the building with his Mum and that's when I realised that I couldn't wait to see him. I hadn't seen him since the morning before and I just wanted to see him. Once I saw him, I knew that I'd know how I felt. I was only going to get to see him as he came down the altar after me. The music started, the song was 'Secret Love Song Part II' by Little Mix, a song that captured everything about the beginning of our relationship, the beginning of our journey together and was so fitting to start our wedding ceremony. As the first chorus began, the door opened and my Mum and I walked into the room. I repeatedly told myself,' look at anyone' and 'focus on looking ahead. I tried to remember to smile as I knew the photographer would be taking pictures, but my main concern was just getting to the front without falling over my shoes.

Then quite quickly, I was at the front with my Mum standing beside me and my back to the window, so I only had my Dad, Mike's Dad and the registrars to look at and to try to forget about the eyes behind looking at me. The door opened again and Mike came in. Yes, I wanted to get married! Yes, I wanted to make this commitment to him! Yes, I wanted to spend the rest of my life with him! I hoped this marriage was going to work! I didn't want to cancel anything and I didn't care if anyone thought we should. As I looked at him and he did that smile he does, I felt every worry, every anxiety and every stressful moment that I had felt leading up to this day be lifted off me. This was all worth it. He had some tears in his eyes too and he forgot to walk down the aisle, instead he walked through the chairs that would have been there if this hadn't been a pandemic wedding. His Mum followed him, she was visibly crying behind her glittery face mask and looked beautiful in her own customised dress. The walk-in didn't take as long as we expected and the song had only gotten to its second verse. I wondered whether we should all stand and just listen to the music but my anxiety of it becoming awkward made me cue my Dad to stop the music.

The ceremony didn't seem as formal as I expected and it was guided a lot by the registrar. I was worried that I wouldn't know what to say and when to say it. The moment came to say our vows that I hadn't yet managed to say without crying and I hadn't yet said them in front of anyone.

"Michael, you are that person in life that I was missing. The person I didn't realise I was waiting for. You came into my life during my darkest time and brought the light that I needed to keep going. I wouldn't be where I am today without you and I doubt I would have been here at all without you. For all these years, you've made me smile, laugh, cry and get mad… a lot. But the main thing you brought was… hope. You made me realise that it's not always battles, hard times and dark moments, and when there is, you'll be there by my side. I'm so proud of how far we have come together, the steps we've made together and the hurdles we have jumped over together. I once asked you to save yourself from what I was going through and you refused. You've always been there for me since. I promise I'll be there for you too, for the rest of our lives… forever."

I had done it. I managed to say them without becoming a blubbering mess and now it was time for Mike to say his vows to me; I had no idea what he was going to say and Mike has never been a man for showing his emotions or telling me how he feels about me.

"I have never been one for words like these in all the years we have been together. From day one, I knew I would struggle if I didn't see you again. As the days, weeks and months went by, it became obvious that I needed you in my life more and more. My life grew and developed with great significance around you. Through the small, big and life-changing steps that were taken, you were always there for me and often gave me the push I needed even in those darker moments. You will forever be the dramatic, impatient one, but you are my dramatic and impatient one and I wouldn't want that to change ever. Every step, breath and move took, I'll always be here, even when you're at your angriest. I will always love, care and support you no matter what life throws at us and I will be here with you right until our older days, but even that won't be the end as this is for eternity. You are my soulmate and soon to be husband. I am truly excited about the next steps in the already fantastic life we have built together. I love you with all my heart."

And then we were pronounced married and for the first time ever, people got to see us kiss. This moment had given me massive anxiety. I had stressed that some people might not want to see two males kissing and it might make them feel uncomfortable, but as the moment happened, all that anxiety had gone and I kissed him with no second thought. The smile that he gave me after we had kissed was one of my favourite moments of the day. It felt really nice to finally be able to finally wear our rings again after not being able to wear them since January. We'd had them engraved then with our original wedding day pre-pandemic, something we still haven't gotten around to having re-done actually. Our parents came to greet us then and hug us and I felt the joining of the two families, as two individuals Mike and I, had brought these two families together. Due to the pandemic, there were moments during the service of sanitising our hands and we weren't able to sign the registry book and instead were given individual forms to sign, but the pandemic didn't dampen our day at all. It was absolutely perfect the way it was. We walked out of the venue holding hands, proudly and smiling away as our guests threw confetti over us, most of it landing in my curly hair. Mike's Gran was on her scooter, so she couldn't throw it above us, but she made sure we got a handful of confetti on us as we approached her, laughing. We had gotten really lucky with the weather for October, but as soon as we began to make our way across the park to take pictures at the bandstand, it began to rain and the umbrellas had to come out. Mike kept an umbrella over me as we walked through the park, chatting about each other's vows, our suits and the morning. We had some pictures taken with our guests before they left for the reception venue, whilst we stayed with the photographer and had some pictures done in the park. The photographer did really well capturing us, I didn't want too many staged photos and as we laughed and chatted to one another, he captured these moments perfectly. In one picture, we are both standing smiling away at one another and it really looks so romantic, but the reality of the moment was that Mike had just told me he had farted and it stunk. The next part of the day was so important to us, probably the most important moment of the day. We needed to go meet up with the dogs to have pictures with them too. Albus and Aurora were staying with their groomer and the photographer kindly drove us to them. They came out to us freshly groomed. Albus had a little bow tie and collar that read "Page Boy". Aurora wore cream flowers around her neck and a black dog nappy (she had started her first season the week before). They ran out to us very excited and not very cooperative for pictures but credit to the photographer, he did amazing to capture some really good pictures of us with them.

 It was on to meet everyone at the wedding reception then, one of our guests had given us the heads up that there was bad traffic on the motorway. We ended up driving through the A Roads, finally arriving at the beautiful restaurant and greeted with a sign that read "Gaskell Wedding" on. This was our surname now. We had a champagne toast in the garden led by Mike's Mum, who nervously and accidentally introduced as "Mr and Mrs Gaskell" instead of Mr and Mr Gaskell. Others may have got offended at this, but I thought it was (excuse my language) fucking hilarious and it completely broke the ice of formality for everybody as we all balled laughing together, the photographer capturing this moment (also on the front cover of the book). Everything was organised really well, the event planner knew which meal was going to each guest and the drinks were flowing nicely. There was only a slight interruption due to the pandemic and that was that only 15 guests could be in the room. However, after a discussion with the event planner, we worked out that the photographer wasn't classed as a guest and he could continue to work and take pictures as the best men did their speeches. Kieran had to stand by the doorway also. Just before we did a dance with our

Mum's, a tray of jagerbombs was passed around and I managed to clumsily spill mine down my shirt, so for the dance I had to keep my suit jacket on to cover up the wet stain. We decided mid-dance with our Mum's that for the last chorus, we would invite our Dad's up to join us and at the end of the song, the six of us huddled together as a united family, that was a moment I couldn't help the tears in my eyes. I'm proud to call everyone that was there that day my family.

The following day we announced our marriage to our remaining family and friends through social media by simply putting a picture the photographer had taken of us in the park laughing away to one another, with the caption as an explanation as to what had happened and how we suffered in silence for the previous six months as our wedding dates were postponed and postponed again. It may not have been the big party reveal that we had originally planned, but it was simple and I liked that and I think it resembled everything we wanted the wedding to be, simply just us two.

They usually say the first year of marriage is the hardest, but I've joked since and said, "throw in two more lockdowns and a pandemic and it's another story altogether." Our married life has so far been stressful, painful and challenging, but as a couple, we are stronger, more knowledgeable and united together. Is our marriage perfect? Far from it. But it's real. I've said for a while now that I don't want the fake relationships that you see on social media anymore. I don't believe in always being happy and everything having to run so perfectly. That's not reality. So I'll take the times of feeling distant, angry and upset because it's outweighed by the support, the laughs and the love we have for one another. Mike is an incredible husband. He is constantly making me laugh, he truly looks after me, especially with the house chores and he makes me feel so loved and supported. I don't mind admitting that I do think he deserves better than me and that I can be a lot for him to handle with my mood swings and all my demons, but he takes it all in his stride and is a terrific support system for me.

I was Joshua Gaskell now and it was time to start a new chapter in my life. I only hoped that I would be leaving my demons behind with Joshua Finch.

CHAPTER THIRTEEN

Shortly after the wedding, it was announced via a television broadcast that the UK would be entering a second lockdown due to the increasing numbers of Covid-19 deaths and infection rates. It meant that our break away in Anglesey had to be cancelled and my business once again had to be closed for the second time. Fortunately, during this national lockdown, it had been made quite clear that it would only be for one month and the aim of the lockdown was so the country could be allowed to celebrate the Christmas holidays with their families, so I didn't worry too much about finances. Although we still had to watch what we spent for the month, we did have some savings left over from the wedding and due to the cancellation of the party and the breakaway to Anglesey. Shortly before the lockdown, I spontaneously decided that after the wedding, I wanted to colour my hair blonde. I think it was because I felt like I needed a fresh start and having blonde hair was one way of finally letting go of Joshua Finch and becoming Joshua Gaskell. However, as I was trying to move on and start afresh, my past began to slowly catch up on me and unfortunately with nothing distracting my view from it anymore I began to slow down and my past was quickly gaining on me. I was able to return to work at the beginning of December. The month was so busy, and the month went so quick that it felt like I had only been back at work two minutes before there was yet another television broadcast announcing that the year 2021 was going, beginning with a third national lockdown.

We did have one thing to look forward to with the start of the new year, as we made the decision to add another puppy. I'd been in contact with this breeder for a while beforehand. Our conversation had started by seeking advice from her on Aurora's first season and eventually led to her telling me she would possibly be having a litter due at the end of 2020. I asked her to keep me informed but I didn't think I would ever be able to win Mike over. Albus was not yet two, Aurora wasn't even one yet, so it seemed mad and reckless to be adding another member to the family, but mad we are. Amos, named of course after another Harry Potter character, was born on 15th December and was able to join our family home in mid-February. He was the perfect addition and has completed our family, as I have to say that I do not think our house can handle any more dogs. I have even joked and said to my friends that if there was ever a contraception pill to stop someone from buying more dogs then I would be happy to take it right now. Three dogs under the age of 2 seriously has kept me busy and very entertained over the third lockdown, but wow, there were many stressful moments, especially when Aurora had just had her operation and she had no concept of resting to heal after her operation.

The third lockdown did change a lot for me. I first noticed that I was beginning to struggle halfway through February but looking back my mental health had been decreasing since January, but being openly honest, my alcohol consumption and recreational drug use had massively increased during this time too. I'm not going to dramatise this and say that I was addicted to drink or drugs. In no way, shape or form was I, but I was drinking and doing cocaine recreationally and I noticed after a few months that it was starting to massively affect my mental health and decided to stop. I can happily say I haven't taken any drugs since making this decision. I know there are some people who do really struggle with drug addiction, I have watched people I know bravely battle their addictions, one friend in particular, who I proudly watch go out of his way to help others with addiction themselves through his social media. He really has been a massive inspiration for telling my own story. I know it can be a very dangerous road to go down and depending on the individual, a very slippery road too. I do not condemn, judge, or look down on anyone who enjoys drinking alcohol or taking drugs. That is completely their choice, but I knew around this time it definitely wasn't helping me, so I stopped and took control before my situation could get any worse. I eventually spoke to my husband and decided that I needed to go back to seeing my therapist again. I hadn't seen a therapist in over a year and I did feel really deflated that I had to go back and that I was back in a position where I felt I had no choice but to accept help from someone else. I have always tried to be very independent when I struggle with my mental health, I usually aim to solve my issues on my own and avoid burdening my husband, friends and family with what I repeatedly go through. How could I be back in this position again? I was meant to have left all my demons behind, I was meant to be a new person, a blonde new person who would no longer struggle with this, but my demons, my negative mind and my self-harming thoughts had all returned. It started off as just a low mood and lack of motivation, but within a few short weeks, my urges to self-harm came back and it took every bit of energy I had to resist these urges. To some, it may seem strange, but I had managed to control these urges for such a long time now, with the very rare relapse in stressful moments. But this time, the urges became more intense and scary. At one point I felt like I wanted to stab myself in the stomach and allow myself to bleed out before Mike would return home from work. The day before my first therapy session with Catherine I had the conversation with a friend about my suppressed memory of when the doctor sexually abused me and it all came to my conscious mind and this time I couldn't push it back anymore. I admitted to my friend what had happened to me and I began the process of acceptance and dealing with the consequences more than ten years later. As I stated earlier in this book, I could not have got through dealing with this without the support of my family and opening up about my experience to my husband, my parents, my brothers and my friends. It has been the most painful but healing experience. I do know what happened to me has affected me. I know it has somehow shaped the person I am today in both positive and negative ways, but it has shaped and developed me into a much stronger person also. I believe that I needed this time in the third lockdown to finally stop and allow myself to struggle, to accept what has happened to me in the past, accept my issues and tackle the origin of all my demons. I still do not feel emotionally or mentally ready to go down the route of reporting the doctor. Maybe in time, I will, but for now, I'm focusing on accepting, dealing and moving on until my mental health is stronger and I'm in a much more stable place. I want to say thank you to those who helped me deal with my demons during the lockdown, especially all my family and the friends that have been there when I needed help to get me through the darkest time of my life.

Only a few weeks after admitting to myself what had happened, my mind went to the darkest possible place and once again, I was having strong and persuasive suicidal thoughts. I was spending all day alone in the house, as Mike still had to work and my mind began to create possible scenarios where I could commit suicide and it be successful. One morning I woke up and the first thought I had was disappointment that I actually had woken up. It was just another day that I had to tackle and another day of being on my own. Mike seemed hesitant about leaving me that morning and he asked if I was going to be ok and I just had to be honest. My answer was, "I don't know". I couldn't promise him that I was still going to be there when he got home from work that day because the reality was, I didn't plan to be. I had planned in my head that I was going to hang myself from the attic that day, but I desperately didn't want Mike to be the person to find me. He didn't deserve to go through that. I had learnt from how my brothers felt after they found me those years before that nobody deserved it. I considered if I should write a note and stick it on the hallway door that would tell him to not come upstairs and instead ring an ambulance and let the paramedics be the ones to find me. But I do know Mike and I know that he wouldn't waste another second waiting for an ambulance and would ignore the note and come running up the stairs and become emotionally scarred for the rest of his life. I just couldn't do that to him, so I fought against the urge with everything I had. Although I fought the suicidal thoughts, I no longer trusted myself to stay at home on my own, so I turned to my Mum and spent my hardest days there with toy parents instead of trying to fight this battle on my own.

I was so grateful for my weekly therapy sessions that I had with Catherine. She understood exactly what I was going through. She understood the character I had developed to protect myself from all the pain and understood the kind of person that I am today. We worked together on understanding and practising safe place meditation and strangely enough, my safe place was under the ocean water, in complete isolation and silence, it is my peaceful state, and this is the place I focus on whenever I meditate, or I am trying to calm myself down, when my mood is low or when my overthinking starts getting the better of me. Catherine suggested that I write a letter to the character I had made all those years ago. I thanked the character for helping get me through some of the most painful times of my life but explained that I was now letting her go as I need to be strong enough to handle the future hard times as myself. When I'm feeling down or frustrated, I listen to podcasts or my favourite music whilst I'm driving in the car, in particular, James Farrelly's 'Free Your Mind' podcast. His podcast and social media inspire me to adapt a new way of thinking and to try to worry less and accept that whatever is meant to just be without over analysing the situation.

As my therapy sessions with Catherine came to an end, she suggested that I wrote this book. She suggested that I should write it all down, write every detail of what I have gone through in my short life and use my experiences to help others. And so, the process of writing this book began. I questioned who would even be interested in anything that I have gone through or anything that I have to say. Who would even care? But I hoped that this book could help anyone who can resonate with it and help them to see that nobody is going through this battle on their own. On the surface, my life may appear to others like a fairytale. Having a family, a husband, the dogs, a house, a business and everything else and it may seem pathetic to some when I say that the reality is that I struggle, I have struggled and still struggle to this day.

I genuinely believe that depression and anxiety are an ongoing war and they require constant work, attention, and dedication. But with the right army, the right tools, the right people and the right influences around you, you can win each battle and take each day as it comes. Throughout my life, I have lost so many people. Some may have passed away, some walked away from me and I've come to understand that this is the pain that I have previously struggled to handle, but I know now that even though the pain of losing someone can be incredibly scary, I have to put my own mental health first because I need to have the right army and influences around me for all my future battles. Ariana Grande released the song "Just Like Magic" and it has the lyric "losing friends left and right but I just send them love and light" and I can relate to that lyric so much in the last 12 months. I have removed many people from life, people who had their own issues to deal with and it was having a negative impact on me, some people that our friendship just lost its purpose, some people who proved they wouldn't be there for me when I needed them, some narcissistic, some manipulative and some controlling people, some that almost took my voice and morals from me and some people that just enjoyed unnecessary drama and conflict and although it has been extremely difficult letting these people go, it has been completely necessary to help me in my battle and their negative influence is no longer hindering or blinding me from a positive mindset. To the people who know that the characters in this book are them and to everyone who has shaped some of the difficult phases of my life, I can only thank you for all the life lessons that you have taught me and I now send you as much light and positive energy as I possibly can and wish you all the best out of life.

I decided to name this book "Puzzle Pieces" halfway through the writing process, as I finally understood that I needed to go through everything that I have gone through in order to be the person that I am today. How would I describe that person? I would describe myself as a very complicated, complex, needy person. I can be a lot for some to handle, but I'm also incredibly hardworking, loving, friendly, protective, passionate about those who I love and I always enjoy trying to make people laugh. I'm currently 25 years old and I'm still growing as an individual and learning about myself every day. Every bad experience, all the pain and all the trauma with all the good memories with friends and family are all puzzle pieces into developing the full picture of who I am today. After completing the process of writing this book, I originally wanted to imagine that I would have finished my puzzle and completed telling my story, but that was an unrealistic view as I'm only young and my puzzle is far from complete. Everything I have experienced so far in life is only the edges to the full picture and the puzzle still needs completing. My therapist asked me during our sessions, "What are you living for?" My answer at the time was only for Mike and my family, especially my Mum, but she wasn't satisfied with my answer to her question and wanted more from me, more passion from me. She asked me to go and find what I wanted to achieve in my life and in all honesty, I really struggled to come up with anything that I wanted to achieve in my life. The only reason that I hadn't attempted to end my life again was because I couldn't destroy Mike or my Mum's life, so what did I have to live for other than that reason? But now I have found a reason. My answer is that I'm living to complete my puzzle. I want to create the most beautiful images for each individual piece to complete the full puzzle. Some of the pieces will be colourful and exciting, some of them will be darker and painful with experiences that are hard to cope with and some will be the darkest shades and outright the most painful experiences of life. I know realistically that I have a lot more painful experiences in life to go through, but I also know that I have the best people around me, the most amazing support and I now allow them to help me when I need it. I know when I need to admit I need their help and together we will all complete our puzzles of life.

For anyone who has read this book, I really do hope that it has helped in some way, no matter how small that may be. I hope that my story has helped you see that you aren't alone in this struggle and that even when everything seems like it's glittering, it isn't always gold. I don't know which of the chapters in this book you related to, but hopefully, we have gone through something similar together and that you can feel like your army is building. Make the most of your life, accept what you have and be grateful for it (writing a small gratitude list really helps build this skill of gratitude and appreciation), start to appreciate those around you rather than push them away, let them love and help you to shine your brightest and keep on fighting in this war against darker times.

A few years ago, my Mum suffered a nervous breakdown and one thing that she did to help keep herself occupied, focused and calm her anxieties was jigsaw puzzles.

I will always be creating my jigsaw puzzle until my last breath and I'm going to need every single piece, the past, the present and the future pieces to create the full picture.

"He picked up the lemons that fate gave him and started a lemonade stand"
—Elbert Hubbard (1915)

Printed in Great Britain
by Amazon